CW00421519

There is much factual
but it does not necess,
standing of them, or th

Your Child and You brings together for the first
time Brenda Crowe's articles on children and
family life that have appeared regularly in
Woman's Realm since 1983. Ranging from visiting the dentist to avoiding sexism, mud pies to
teenage insights; through sympathetic observation and often humorous anecdotes, she dis-
cusses the hopes and fears of parenthood, the
demands and joys of the family, and ways of
encouraging parents to help themselves and
their children to make the most of this complex
but ultimately rewarding relationship.

Your Child and You features examples of daily
family life with which everyone can identify –
helping us to remember and use constructively
the experiences of our own childhood. Without
attempting to provide unrealistic answers,
Brenda Crowe's warm approach offers many
suggestions for ways in which families can
interact, accept and support each other.

Brenda Crowe was for ten years the National
Adviser to the Pre-School Playgroups Association, and her remarkable ability to observe and
comment on all aspects of family life is now well
known through her work as author and TV and
radio broadcaster.

Your Child and You

BRENDA CROWE

London
UNWIN PAPERBACKS
Boston   Sydney

First published in Great Britain by Unwin Paperbacks 1986
This book is copyright under the Berne Convention. No reproduction
without permission. All rights reserved.

UNWIN ® PAPERBACKS
40 Museum Street, London WC1A 1LU, UK

Unwin Paperbacks
Park Lane, Hemel Hempstead, Herts HP2 4TE

George Allen & Unwin Australia Pty Ltd
8 Napier Street, North Sydney, NSW 2060, Australia

Unwin Paperbacks with the Port Nicholson Press
PO Box 11-838 Wellington, New Zealand

British Library Cataloguing in Publication Data

Crowe, Brenda
Your child and you.
1. Child rearing   2. Parent and child
I. Title
306.8′74   HQ769
ISBN 0-04-649039-6

Set in Linotron 202 Palatino
by Pardy Printers, Ringwood, Hampshire
Made and printed in Great Britain by the
Guernsey Press Co. Ltd., Guernsey, Channel Islands.

Acknowledgement

With gratitude to Vera Hughes who broke into her happy retirement to continue both typing and our friendship by post.

Contents

INTRODUCTION

In 1983 I was asked if I would like to contribute a regular weekly to *Woman's Realm* called *Your Child and You*. The thought was daunting, but sometimes these things decide themselves just because they feel right – and this was one of those times.

There is a great deal of factual information about children, but this doesn't necessarily add up to understanding – and it is often the misunderstandings which arise between parents and children that lead to frustration on both sides. Where better to share hints, tips and insights than in a magazine which is based on the premise that 'the quality of family life matters most'?

The first articles were short and tentative, and I wondered how long it would be before I ran out of ideas. I needn't have worried, for the readers took over and nudged me into the deeper waters of family relationships and self-awareness.

I am deeply indebted to the writers of letters which came from mothers and fathers, grandmothers and grandfathers, teenagers, concerned friends and relations, students, lecturers, teachers, health visitors, social workers, a store detective, a road safety officer, a patient in a psychiatric hospital and men and women from all walks of life who had memories and observations to offer.

My role has become that of go-between, first and foremost trying to speak on behalf of the youngest children who can't speak for themselves – but simultaneously trying to link the observable child to the child still hidden within us all.

Some readers have made their own books from the cut-out articles, and many have asked if a book is available – so here it is, in the hope that others will also be able to say with growing confidence, 'But I know that . . . only I didn't know that until I read it', or 'It's only commonsense really . . .' Occasionally you may pick up a helpful hint or tip – or disagree, and clarify your own thoughts further in doing so.

It isn't a book to read, but rather to dip into. You won't find any 'answers', but perhaps memories will begin to stir which give you the insight and excitement to watch and listen to your children as though they were yourself when young – whether your children are 'terrible-twos' at school, out in the world, or parents in their turn.

PART ONE

THE DEPTH AND BREADTH OF PARENTHOOD

PARENTS' HOPES AND RESPONSIBILITIES

For many years now I have been asking groups of parents what they most want for their children, and never once has their answer varied: without even stopping to think they say in unison, 'Health and happiness.'

The next question is, 'Anything else . . .?', and at this point comes a pause for thought before someone says hesitantly, as though perhaps it isn't quite the done thing to voice such hopes in this day and age, 'Well . . . I hope one day they'll get married, and have children . . . and if they do, I hope it will be a happy marriage.' A sea of nodding heads reassures the speaker, who then adds for the benefit of those who aren't nodding, 'But only if they want to . . . people don't have to marry these days . . . it isn't right for everyone.'

Someone else then invariably says, to more nodding of heads all round, 'I'd like them to have a really good education, and to *learn*; it doesn't have to be university, they can be hairdressers or nurses or work in an office – it's *wanting* to do the job, and learning to do it well, that matters.'

As always ordinary parents, who are the backbone of the country, have hit the nail on the head. They know that they want to bring up children who are positively well and happy; who enjoy 'doing' rather than being looked-after and waited-on; who have the courage to make loving relationships, even though suffering is an inescapable part of love; and who believe that if a job is worth doing, it is worth doing properly – be it washing-up, managing a bank, looking after elephants at the zoo, or learning to be a parent.

The trouble is that whilst wanting these things parents often find it very hard to help their children confront the experiences that may be painful – they want to alleviate pain and suffering too soon, or prevent it altogether, rather than to stand by with loving support while their children go through the experience and come out the other side stronger and wiser. But love must be strong as well as compassionate.

3

Parents also often find it hard to help their children to become responsible, independent and sharing partners in the family; the example of our own parents, or guilt, or need, or desire, leads so many of us to feel that we 'ought' to know and be the answer to all our children's questions and problems; that we 'ought' to be wholly responsible for all the shopping, cooking, cleaning, maintenance and budgetting; and that we 'ought' to be the ones who know best about everything, all the time. Certainly children shouldn't be drudges, but they *need* to feel useful and necessary, as well as loved, members of the family.

One of the most valuable sources of help available to all parents lies within us. If we look back down the years it is possible to pinpoint the people who made an impact on our lives – for better and worse. We can try to recall the relatives who stimulated, frightened or bored us; the teachers who fired us with enthusiasm, and those who killed all joy in their subject; the people who made us feel happy and confident, and those who lowered our self-esteem to vanishing point; the friends of both sexes who fired us into a new orbit, and those who used us as fuel for their own rocket before taking-off into orbit themselves and jettisoning us (or did we fall away because life had made us expect to be losers?).

We need to try to recapture our *feelings*, for our children will go through every single one of them.

The other, and most important source of learning of all, is our children – if only we will take the time *really* to listen, and *really* to see. But only then if we can link what we see, hear and sense, to what we know from our own experience.

Try for just one day to monitor yourself and your background feelings, and to say to yourself at intervals, 'I'm happy' – and make a mental or written note of what you are doing. Happiness can come with a letter, or a job well done, or a burst of sun, or a successful purchase or transaction, or for no reason at all. Also note those times when you say to yourself, 'I'm upset, my inside is doing uncomfortable things, and I'm shaking' – what caused it? Likewise, 'I feel useful, needed and appreciated' – what were you doing, how much of the satisfaction came with the job itself, and how much in the reaction of others?

Learn to know the sources of your own honest feelings, then spend the next day watching your child (one day for each child), and compare notes with your partner, your parents, your in-laws and your friends. What *does* make people happy? In spite of differences in temperament, age, and stage of life, you will probably find that the sources of happiness, unhappiness, fear and confidence, satisfaction and frustration, and a heightened or lowered self-esteem are common to us all. In understanding this it is possible to see more clearly where our responsibilities lie if we want our children to grow up to be happy, healthy in mind and body, loving and giving in relationships (without being a doormat or a martyr), and capable of working at any relationship or job which comes to hand – whether it be paid employment, voluntary work, a hobby, or the vital job of rearing a family.

KEEPING PROMISES

A promise is a source of great comfort and security as long as it carries with it the absolute assurance that we will do, or not do, give or not give, say or not say, exactly what we promise.

If promises are lightly given and easily broken they cease to have any value, and we are left with nothing solid to offer our children to sustain them in times of real need. Perhaps even more damaging is the fact that if we lose our children's trust, we also begin to lose their respect.

We have all made and broken promises, let people down, and let ourselves down in our own eyes. But that doesn't mean we shouldn't go on trying to learn to do better, especially in this matter of promises to children.

Think carefully before you make a promise, and only commit yourself when you feel you can stand by your word no matter what happens.

You may promise an ice-cream when the van comes round. But the van may break down, or be sold out of anything but big blocks which you can't afford on that particular day; it isn't your fault, but in the child's mind a promise has been broken.

You may promise to take your child to the park '. . . this afternoon, if you just let me get on and finish this now', but by the afternoon it may be pouring with rain or an unexpected visitor may call; it isn't your fault, but your promise has been broken. In good faith, and after serious thought about all the responsibilities and complications involved, you may promise a guinea pig for a birthday present; but circumstances over which you have no control may mean you have to move into a flat where pets are not allowed. Yet another promise is broken.

Children are sticklers for detail, and they won't hold us to anything unreasonable if we haven't used the magic word, but if we have, then they will turn on us and say, 'But you promised!'

If the word is to hold the certainty that children need we must be very careful about what we promise. In our family this came down to three things. We promised we would never stop loving them (even if we didn't like them sometimes); never to leave them alone in the house when they were in bed (not even to get the washing in from the garden); and never to stop looking for them if they were lost.

Only you know what reassurance your children need, and you can manage. It doesn't matter how much or how little that may be, as long as it is honest.

ACCEPTING CHILDREN'S 'GOOD IDEAS'

Few experiences are as disheartening as having all your helpful suggestions thrown back in your face. It seems there are some people who just can't be helped, and no matter how hard we try we are slapped down every time. In the end we just give up trying, sometimes regretfully but occasionally with the inner comment, 'Oh, get on with it yourself then.'

If we aren't careful we can do exactly the same thing to children. They have an endless succession of 'good ideas', which they put into practice then and there – quite often to give us a lovely surprise – only to find that we rebuff them.

I can remember so many ideas that were 'good' from the

child's point of view, even though they were 'bad' for those who had to cope with the consequences.

There was the child who had a lovely weekend gardening with his parents, and wanting to carry on with the good work on Monday morning he watered the flowers on the living room carpet with his watering can.

And the child who carried milk bottles in, only to fall on the step breaking one of them. The first her mother knew of it was when one intact, and one broken, milk bottle were brought to her in the kitchen. The child misread anxiety for displeasure and before her mother could say anything chipped in with, 'It's all right, I've mopped it up with my knickers.'

I can remember being told to 'wash the watercress well', so I rubbed it with carbolic soap.

We are only human, and there will be times when we can't refrain from saying, 'Look what you've done!' But children would find learning so much easier if we could follow that up with, 'I'm sorry I was cross. You were trying to help, and it was a very good idea you had, but there was something you didn't know about, so let me explain . . .'

If children are to go on trying to please and help us it is important that we adopt as many of their ideas as we can, otherwise they will give up trying. We can encourage them by asking for their advice – and accepting it, even if they do suggest sardine sandwiches and chocolate spread for tea, or a picnic on the stairs to enliven a wet day.

TALKING TO CHILDREN

Children are very responsive to our voices, and react to our tone and mood long before they understand what we are saying. This is why they need us to talk to them from birth onwards; when they cry it is comforting to be picked up and to hear a soothing voice saying, 'I know, you're wet and dirty and uncomfortable, but we'll soon have you nice and warm and clean and dry.' They learn that when we talk it is a signal that we are communicating something to their advantage, and the habit of listening and responding is encouraged.

Babies soon begin to discover sounds, and if we repeat them they will gradually give them back to us again. And understanding grows that sounds are a two-way communication.

Eventually names are connected to objects, and if we say 'Milk?' there is an excited bouncing up and down. Repeated sounds are slowly mastered. Dad-dad-dad usually precedes mum-mum-mum, and although they may have begun as experimental sounds, parental joy and response is so great that there is an added incentive to connect these sounds with two very important people. Other naming words follow – cat, car, dog – or the nearest derivative that they can manage – bikki or bikket, boon (spoon), 'tato or buppy (bread and butter). This is not baby talk in the sense that so offends some parents, it is a serious attempt to reproduce a word or phrase that the ears, brain, lips, tongue and vocal cords cannot yet combine to produce correctly. Any attempt to 'correct' their pronunciation is likely to set up anxiety, and may delay rather than help the process of learning to speak. Rather, agree with the child and just repeat the word correctly yourself, 'Yes, bread and butter. Nice!' Or they may invent their own words, but accept them because if they are constant then they are genuinely communicating and need to know that we understand.

Then comes the ability to string words together – 'Daddy car', 'Peter milk' (most refer to themselves by name for quite a long time) or 'Peter beed' which is understandable as a shortened version of 'I, Peter, have sat upon the pot and had the good luck to do what you wanted me to do.' The tenses of verbs will be muddled for some time yet, but just indicate your pleasure at both the announcement and the deed by repeating, 'Yes, you have been a clever boy, haven't you?'

Some children start talking intelligently in their second year, others may say almost nothing by the beginning of their third year and yet give every indication that they hear and understand perfectly well. Sometimes this is due to the fact that everyone else in the family anticipates their every need, and therefore there is no need to ask. Sometimes they may have been bored into defensive silence by adults carrying them round and pointing to every object in sight saying, 'Picture! Can you say picture? Telephone! Tell-ee-ffone . . .

What is it? Tell-ee . . .?' Speech needs to be acquired slowly by experiment, copying, experience and association – with the reward of discovering that words create bonds between people. If they create barriers, then the message received may be, 'It's best to keep still and quiet, then I shan't be nagged or scolded.' Never punish along the lines of, 'You can't have it until you ask for it properly'; always build on success and let them know you understand, or are trying to understand, so that their confidence in being able to communicate is boosted.

Some slow starters suddenly begin to talk in complete sentences, others talk so quickly that they fall over the words in their eagerness to communicate; go down to their level, smile to share their excitement, and say, 'Slowly . . . tell me again.' The fact that you can't dash off quickly from that position often enables them to slow down.

But if, by about 2½, a child is not beginning to use words easily, then put your mind at rest by seeing your health visitor or doctor. They can arrange for a full assessment at a Paediatric Assessment Centre. If help is needed it can be arranged, but if you are assured that speech development is a little slower than usual but is within acceptable limits, then you can relax and not allow friends or relations to pressure you into a state of anxiety which may affect your child.

The Association for All Speech Impaired Children will help you if you have any difficulties. (See *Useful Addresses*.)

LEARNING TO APOLOGISE

All of us sometimes do or say something we regret. Usually it is just thoughtlessness – the words are out or the deed is done before we see what the consequences are likely to be. Or we lash out at someone or something with a reaction that is out of all proportion to the provocation, just because we were feeling at odds with ourself anyway, and something quite minor triggered the explosion. Whatever the cause, when it has been our fault, most of us are able to say immediately, 'I'm sorry. I didn't mean it', and are so distressed that forgiveness is offered readily.

Some people aren't able to apologise at the time; although many want to, the words just stick in their throats. As one mother said, 'I don't know why, but I just can't say the words, "I'm sorry". I'm getting a bit better, if I bump into someone and it's my fault I can say "sorry!" now instead of, "Look where you're going!" But I could never, ever say I'm sorry to my husband or children – and they are the ones I most want to say it to. I'm awful sometimes. I don't mean to be, but the words just come out. And afterwards I'm so ashamed that I can't do anything about it – I just want to forget it. I'll make them a specially nice meal, and then they know it's over.'

Others can't apologise at the time, and making amends by a nice meal wouldn't be enough for them – it would leave them still feeling guilty, For their own peace of mind they have to find a time when they can say the words, 'I'm sorry', and above all they need to hear the words, 'It's all right.' Forgiveness is needed before they can feel right with themselves again. This is how it is for most of us.

There is often a connection between those who can't apologise, and a childhood in which they received little or no comfort or understanding; it was nagging, shouting and punishments all the way. According to temperament children tend to react to this in one of two ways. Some lose confidence and self-esteem to the point where they feel worthless; and the final demand, 'Now say you're sorry!' after one of their transgressions, meets with the silence of fear – not 'stubbornness' but the real fear that if they say these words they are finally admitting to themselves that they are worthless beyond redemption. Others, of a more robust constitution, 'know' from quite an early age that they are not going to allow anyone, not even parents, to rob them of their own feeling of self-worth. And if these children are told to say they are sorry when they don't feel any regret for what they have done, then nothing will make them, not even threats or punishments. This is 'stubborn', according to the dictionary meaning of 'unyielding, not docile or amenable to control', but before condemning it we should search ourselves. Why should we force a child to express dishonest feelings? Emotional dishonesty is the cause of a great deal of suffering in later life, and it begins in childhood if we are made to feel ashamed or guilty of our real feelings.

The sad thing is that those parents who had a harsh childhood are likely to find it hardest to apologise, and yet find themselves inflicting the same pattern on their children – complete with demands for apologies. If you know yourself to be caught in this trap, don't despair. There is quite a simple trick which often works: start to practise making apologies *before* anything happens – 'Sorry, love, I nearly trod on your toe!' This builds up goodwill, and then when it really does happen it is easier to say, 'Sorry! Was that your toe?' rather than to wait for the wail and then say, 'Well, you shouldn't get under my feet.'

It is up to us to set the example, and establish the habit both of apologising and, just as important, accepting the apologies of others.

We also need to examine that common habit of advancing upon children who are awash with the aggression, guilt or the fear of the moment, and demanding, 'Now say you're sorry!' I often saw the result of such an approach in the nursery schools where I worked. There were always some children who were aggressive, and often a wail of pain, rage or distress would go up from a victim, and as I went over to see what was happening the culprit would cower away, or stand his ground, saying urgently, 'I've said I'm sorry!' In other words, he had got the message that you were free to do as you liked as long as you immediately said the magic password.

Sometimes we even forget that children may not yet grasp that the word 'sorry' has different meanings under different circumstances. If we have been in the wrong, then 'I'm sorry' is an apology and a request for forgiveness; if a child's guinea pig dies, then 'I'm sorry' is an expression of sympathy.

We also overlook the fact that sometimes a child has every justification to feel angry – his painstakingly built castle is knocked down, and he lashes out with a spontaneity that can't yet be controlled. In this case it might be more appropriate to say, 'I saw what happened, no wonder you felt angry, but I think it was an accident. Shall we both help you to build it up again?'

All children are sometimes thoughtless, careless or unkind in the heat or ignorance of the moment, and are then suddenly confronted with the consequences of their actions – the cup is broken, the baby is screaming with a lump on his head, or the bathroom basin is overflowing and we're pounding up the stairs. We forget how frightening such moments can be; they would say 'Elephants' if we demanded it, and it would mean just about as much as our expected 'I'm sorry'. Better, really, for everyone to calm down, and then say they are sorry when they really mean it. 'I'm sorry' should be the expression of true feelings if it is to mean anything.

HELPING CHILDREN TO LEAVE HOME AND PARENTS OCCASIONALLY

During teacher training we saw various forms of provision for the under-fives, and one visit still stands out in my memory. It was a day spent in a residential nursery, and as soon as I sat down among the children they were all over me. They scrambled on my lap, hung round my neck, clutched my hands, and sat at my feet hugging my legs. I gloried in it, it was so flattering, and I felt more than a little smug at my magnetic attraction for children. At the end of the day our tutor talked it all over with us, and said to me, 'Did you understand how promiscuous those children were? They are so starved of the love of one central person in their lives that they have to make-do with getting the attention and physical contact of anybody who is available.'

Many years later at the Child Guidance Clinic I met the opposite. A boy of 8 couldn't be prised away from his mother, who adored him and was as distressed at the idea of parting as he was. Eventually the explanation came, 'When he was born the midwife put him into my arms and said, "All he needs is love. You can't love him too much." We're never apart. I lie beside him every night holding his hand until he falls asleep, so whatever is wrong I *know* it isn't lack of love.'

What *was* lacking was the understanding that love isn't endless emotion and togetherness.

Between these two extremes comes an endless variation on the theme of separation. Sometimes a child is particularly confident by the age of 3 or 4, and after only one or two previous visits to a playgroup with his mother is prepared to leave her without a backward glance on his first day there. And suddenly it may be the mother who loses confidence and thinks, 'He can't love me as much as I love him, or he wouldn't find it so easy to leave me.' And almost subconsciously she calls out, 'I'll be back at 12 o'clock . . . you'll be all right, won't you? . . . I shan't be long . . . I'm coming back.' And suddenly the child wavers and thinks, 'She's coming back? It never occurred to me that she wouldn't . . . but suppose she gets lost, or forgets me?' Confidence wavers, and back he rushes to cling to her.

All might have been well if someone had been there to say to the mother at the beginning, 'What a lovely confident child. You must be very pleased with yourself.'

Many children have a more sensitive constitution; and others can't be rushed into anything without a long period of preparation; and most simply haven't had enough experience of brief periods of separation for them to know with absolute certainty that 'going' is always followed by 'coming back'. And even when they 'know' the moment of parting is still painful.

'She'll be all right once you've gone' people say cheerily, or 'The tears never last for long', or 'The quicker you go the better', or 'Slip out when she's not looking'. I sometimes wonder how these people would feel if they were taken to a hospital for an operation – a completely new experience in an unfamiliar environment – and were dumped on the doorstep with their suitcases and a cheery 'Bye bye'.

Some of us have had hospital experience more than once, and still get that slight sinking feeling, that bleak moment when we get out of our clothes and see them taken away; parting with shoes and coats seems so final.

Children are helpless and powerless in a world still strange and geared to knowledgeable adults. Why should we dismiss their nervousness and distress as being less than our own? If we stay with them in friends' houses or playgroups for as long as they need us their moment for parting will eventually arrive. And if it doesn't we can say, 'All right, let's go home together and come another day' (never slip away unnoticed, that is a betrayal of trust). If they know they are free to stay or leave with us they feel safer, and the day will come when we can say, 'I'm just going to do some shopping, do you want to stay or come with me?' and they will prefer to stay (especially if you leave them your handbag and take only your purse).

There is no hurry. If each stage is taken slowly the foundations of security will last them all their lives.

Once parents understand the need to stay with a child who is faced with a new environment, with unfamiliar people, and unknown routines, they can often plan to stay as part of the settling-in process for the first few times at least. But sometimes there are circumstances which make it impossible – if so, explain beforehand, give assurances that you will be back, and be early rather than late. And sometimes, with the best of intentions, courage wavers in the face of someone saying, 'Go quickly . . . it's best for the child' – but try to be firm. Learning to separate is as hard for the parent as it is for the child, and both gain from it being a gradual process.

LETTING CHILDREN EXPERIENCE THE DIRECT CONSEQUENCE OF THEIR ACTIONS WHEN POSSIBLE

The other day I met someone I hadn't seen for some time, and we stopped to exchange news of our families. Just as we were about to part she said, 'I must tell you one more thing, I'm so thrilled about it.' I understood exactly why she felt as she did, and have her permission to pass on the story.

Her dearly loved daughter and son-in-law have two children, a boy of 13 we'll call Alan, and a girl of 11 we'll call Ann. Both children are the apples of their Grandmother's eye, happy, loving, kind, thoughtful, 'But sometimes they can be a bit . . . well, you know what children are . . . especially as they get older.'

On the occasion in question it was a Saturday and the family was at home, all happily pottering about and doing what they wanted to do. Potatoes in their jackets were baking in the oven, and around midday the mother – we'll call her

Daphne – stopped doing what she was getting on with so satisfactorily and went into the kitchen to prepare a salad. She called out to Alan, said that the meal would soon be ready, and asked him if he would set the table. It was one of those days, and after a series of grumbles and excuses he blurted out, 'No, I don't feel like it,' and disappeared.

Since these parents were not the sort to insist on blind obedience just for the sake of it, she let it pass on this occasion, and repeated the request to Ann. But the younger one had just reached the stage of being influenced by her brother, and with a new spirit of daring she ranged herself alongside him and announced, 'I don't feel like it, either!' and scuttled off.

Daphne thought for a bit. At this stage you can neither let things slip through weakness, or indifference, or because it is easier and quicker to do the job yourself; nor can you 'force' children to set a table. And the issue involved wasn't nearly important enough to be allowed to escalate into a fully fledged battle of wits and wills.

She pondered for a bit, and then suddenly knew exactly what she was going to do, and did it with the peace of mind which comes with this sort of 'knowing'. She set two trays, washed half a lettuce and two tomatoes, and prepared two meals. Then she called to her husband, 'Paul, dinner's ready.' He came down, found her in the kitchen, was told quickly and quietly what was afoot, he winked his agreement, and they both carried their trays through to the living room.

A few minutes later they heard the children hurtle downstairs and go into the dining room. There was a pause, then they could be heard going into the kitchen. Then they burst into the living room, stopping in their tracks at the unaccustomed sight of their parents eating in armchairs. Alan said, 'Where's our dinner?', and Daphne calmly said, 'I didn't feel like getting it.'

At this point the narrator couldn't contain her glee: 'When Daphne told me she said, "You should have seen their faces. I didn't go on at them, I just gave them back their own words – we could see it registering, and they couldn't say a thing!"'

Alan recovered his composure first and retaliated with, 'I shall go down to the Windmill', to which his mother replied, 'You can't, you haven't got any money – and I'm certainly not going to give you any.' He tried again, 'Well, all right, I'll go and open some baked beans', but again Daphne countered with, 'You'll do no such thing – I'm not having my store cupboard raided when there is food already available. If you're hungry you can have what we're having. The potatoes are in the oven, the sliced meat is on the dish, and you can wash yourselves some lettuce and tomatoes.'

Ann, who had been shocked speechless by the unexpected repercussions of their modest mutiny, rallied and asked, 'Can we have ours on trays with you?' And Paul said cheerfully, 'Not on your life! We don't want spills in here – go and set the table.'

So they did, later, but infinitely wiser, than at the first request.

AVOIDING SEXISM

It was more than time for the 'dolls for girls, trains for boys' convention to be tossed away, but not if it is to be flipped to 'trains for girls, dolls for boys', for that is just the reverse side of a counterfeit coin.

Conventions are deep rooted, and whilst most parents don't mind saying of their daughters, 'She's a real tomboy!', many are quite irrationally worried if they can't say of their sons, 'He's a real boy!' Anxiety, and false expectations about sex can do such harm in these early years that I would like to try to explain some of the groundless worries.

The most important point to grasp is that young children are *people* rather than boys or girls. Think of a seedbed – the first seed-leaves bear no resemblance to the leaves which will come later, yet we don't have to worry about each plant's identity for it is already genetically determined. All we have to do is give the seedlings the conditions in which they can, in their own time, grow towards what they are. Once the plants are firmly established, then we can supply supports and a minimum of pruning and training, as long as this is in harmony with the species' natural growth.

So it is with children. They all need *exactly* the same chances as each other to establish themselves in a totally new and complex world – free of our sexual interpretations of their play and characteristics.

Consider colour, which is one of the joys of life. Children are drawn to colour as naturally as bees, unless they are told that 'Pink is for girls, blue is for boys. Boys mustn't want pink things, but it's perfectly all right for girls to want blue as well as pink things.' Put like this the absurdity is obvious, yet small boys are still not only being denied one of nature's loveliest colours, but made to feel guilty about a perfectly natural preference.

Colour psychologists are becoming fashionable, but surely we all know what different colours do to us, and for us, at different times and under different circumstances? So do children, and they should be left free to respond to colours just as we do, unencumbered by our psychological or sexual interpretations if they get hooked on black or pink!

Another anxiety is doll play for boys. Toy manufacturers were quick to latch on to the fact that those who work with children know that doll play is as natural for boys as for girls, if they want it, but that some parents are allergic to boys playing with dolls. So they produced Action Man and other boy-dolls. This is better than no dolls, but it misses the point that doll play simply isn't sexist.

We all learn by imitation, and children copy their parents in order to 'feel' what it is like to be a mother *and* a father. In just the same way they try out what it feels like to be a cat lapping milk, or a car in full sound and motion, but that doesn't worry us, does it?

Doll play has a deeper significance, too. There are times when *all* children may need to say and do to dolls what they would like to do and say to their parents, if only they dared. They are not just 'playing with dolls'; play as nature prompts is a way of releasing pressure and helping them to resolve problems. They are learning to cope with their feelings about adults in a safe and manageable way, because they are in control over dolls, who can't react other than in the child's imagination.

Dolls also provide an outlet for the protective feelings which should be, and remain, part of every man and woman. Also a safe outlet for the hostile feelings they have towards the baby sometimes, so think twice before saying 'Poor dolly, don't stamp on her like that, pick her up and love her.' Children sometimes need one doll or toy to ill-treat as a safe outlet for strong feelings.

They can also be compensation, particularly for a child who feels required to grow-up or be big before he or she is ready. If they feel short of loving acceptance and cherishing, then they will often give a doll what they really want for themselves. It is a cry for security that should be heeded.

Boys dressing-up in women's clothes also worries some parents, and they have secret fears that their son might be a transvestite in the making; do be comforted, they are just dressing-up.

They have to learn everything from scratch, about colour, shape, size and the 'feel' of various clothes, especially of those different from their own; the 'feel' of trousers, short and long skirts, flowered hats and cloth caps, wedding dresses and batman's cloaks. They enjoy the different 'feel' of themselves as they look in the mirror, or play in their favouite garb of the moment. It isn't 'dressing up in women's clothes' that is damaging, it is the guilt put upon the child by parental attitudes. Keep a dressing-up box of 'women's clothes' and jewellery, but also colourful football jerseys, 'men's' hats and helmets and uniforms and invite other children to play.

Parents also worry if their sons say they want to cut off their 'willies' and be flat like their mothers, and if their daughters say they want a 'willie', or even ask if theirs has been cut off. This is a perfectly natural stage of learning about their own, and their parents' bodies, and shouldn't be interpreted as castration wishes or penis envy or any other psychological phenomena. Just answer their comments and questions, and give friendly, unemotional, explanations.

If, after all this, you still feel concerned about your child, then do make an appointment at the Child Guidance Clinic – for your own peace of mind, for your worries may be affecting your child more than you realize. And it just may be that there is something in your own relationship with one or other of your own parents that needs to be resolved. Our own early conditioning leaves us all with unresolved problems of one kind or another, and we can project these on to our children; it is a relief for everyone if we can be set free before we pass the negative aspects of our own childhood on to our children.

Our parents weren't always right – how could they be? They had parents of their own to contend with, and an era of their own with which to be in tune. It is a sign of maturity, not disloyalty, to look back and re-assess our childhood, as long as we do it without blame, and remember all the good things, too.

RELEASING CHILDREN FROM GUILT

All of us can surely remember those times when our consciences were heavy with wrong-doing, and we longed to own-up to ease the burden, but didn't dare.

For some children it is fear of the consequence that holds them back. They can't face the anger, blame, withering scorn or sarcasm that experience tells them will be their lot. Many children will tell you that they don't mind punishment – being sent to their rooms, being kept in, losing a privilege – as long as they are not shouted at, which upsets them more than anything else.

For other children, particularly those who are over-protected, it is often fear of losing love that keeps them silent. They are so aware of their parents' generosity and goodness that they feel, 'How could they possibly go on feeling the same about me now that I've done this?' The 'this' will vary as they grow older, but the anxiety doesn't lessen; always it is 'Last time they were able to forgive that, but this is so much worse.'

Then there are the children who could and would own-up, if only they knew what it was that was troubling them, but they have pushed it down so deep that it isn't consciously available. The first sign that something is wrong may be the onset of physical symptoms – a headache, tummy ache, sickness or breathing difficulties. It is no help at all to say, 'There's nothing wrong with you, so off you go to school', because there *is* something wrong if the dread of school, playgroup or a friend's house is so great that it expresses itself physically. The answer is to uncover the fear, and work out how to cope with it, not to deny its very existence. But pinpointing fears can be difficult, especially if the answer to 'What's the matter?' is 'Nothing.'

Sometimes a child will go off to school quite happily, but come back at the end of the day upset. If tea, play and a bath doesn't restore confidence, then it can help to sit on the end of the bed and follow the day through with slow encouragement: 'You were fine when you went off this morning, was it still all right when you got to school?' If the answer is Yes then go on slowly, waiting for as long as is necessary for the answers, 'Was it still all right at Assembly . . .? During the first lessons . . .? At break . . .?' When the tension mounts, and the responses slow down, you can say, 'Good, I think we're getting near now, don't you?' Make it an exercise in togetherness, and when the moment is pinpointed say, 'Well done, you've found it.' For it is indeed well done when we can identify and share what is troubling us, and it is also halfway to healing. But whatever comes to light must be accepted calmly, otherwise the trust won't be there for the next time.

The child may admit to having cheated in class, in which case the most helpful response is, 'I know, I remember doing that, either because I was frightened of being wrong, or couldn't face saying that I still didn't understand. Which was it for you?' Or the trouble may be bullying, and it isn't much help to say, 'Hit him back!' because the child would probably have done that spontaneously if he could – and if he can't (because of our gentle upbringing, or bullying?) it heightens the feeling of inadequacy. Try to work out together practical ways of avoiding the difficult encounters as a first step to gaining confidence to tackle them. And don't betray the confidence without permission.

Another way of releasing children from unhappy silence is to start at the top and work down. Try, 'Well, have you accidentally killed anyone?' If the answer is a vigorous No then go on to, 'Well, did you accidentally set fire to the school? . . . Or find a diamond ring and forget to hand it in to the headmaster or a policeman?' When we seem prepared to take any of these things in our stride it is easier for them to get their own misdeeds in perspective, and 'telling' becomes possible.

It is worth reminding ourselves that we all have accidents, make mistakes, do and say silly things, and acquit ourselves badly in our own eyes or the eyes of others. What matters is not what happens, but how it is coped with – and for that our children need us to be both a friend and a good example.

But having said all that, we must recognise children's needs to keep part of their lives private from us. Parents should never pry – we must do no more than try to be aware of those times when children seem to want to tell us something, but need us to make an opening.

ASSESSING THE EFFECT OF SHOUTING

There is no way any of us is going to get through life without being shouted at. The spontaneous shout for safety is essential, the occasional shout of exasperation is natural and healthy, but habitual shouting is both pointless and damaging.

The whole question of shouting has come to interest me very much since I started making enquiries into children's fears some years ago. It isn't the spider-type of fears that concern me as much as those intangible fears which erode happiness and inhibit learning.

As part of my enquiry I asked the assistance of a teacher of 13–15-year-old boys in a tough urban area. It turned out that shouting figured prominently in their anonymous written comments. Under the heading 'What frightens you at home?' they wrote (with their own spelling): 'I am frightened when my dad or mam shout at me'; 'When my mum shouts I am frightened'; 'When my dad shouts I am frightened'; 'When my dad shouts at me I feel skared'; 'When mam and dad shout at each other'; 'When she shouts at us'; 'When my dad shouts it frightens me'; 'Shouting'; 'When they shout'; 'Shouting at me and belting me'; 'When my father shouts at me, but not when they hit me because I know it is for a reason.'

In talking with other teenagers this same point emerges – they don't mind being punished nearly as much as they mind being shouted at. Their school-based comments were much the same: 'I'm frightened when they're shouting at me'; 'Shouting at me'; 'My teacher scares me because she shouts'; 'Mr. A when he shouts'; 'Miss when she shouts'; 'I'm frightened when any teacher shouts at me or the class.'

Taking into consideration their other comments, and bearing in mind the location of the school and the pressure the parents are under, it is clear these children live in an atmosphere of violence. But it is also clear that among the countless causes they have for fear – attacks by parents and bigger boys, punishments, horror stories and films, handing in homework, sitting exams, harrowing experiences – being shouted at has a particular dread of its own. I begin to wonder whether fear of loud noises (which, together with the fear of falling, is one of the few instinctive fears we all have) plays some part in this?

Whatever the reasons we would all do well to remember that this type of fear has the power to make you 'start to feel swetty', 'go all cold', 'feel inn tense and tremble', 'get a lomp in my throat', 'feel tremblish', 'my tummy goes funny', 'your heart beats very fast', 'I go tense and feel hungry'. Isn't that just what happens to most of us when we are shouted at?

Most of us may feel confident that we are not habitual shouters, but are aware that we shout under certain circumstances. Relief is one – our child narrowly escapes being run over, and our fear is released as anger. Not only do we shout, but shake and slap as well sometimes. And I'm not sure that this is a bad thing; we release emotions that are too strong to be controlled, and our child has that particular lesson well and truly reinforced, as long as we then calm each other down, and then explain what it was all about.

The other shout-inducing occasions are those confrontations with our growing children when we want (and need) to express our disapproval, and they won't listen/don't admit/can't see what we are driving at. In short, when we aren't winning, and that fact in itself may be more important to us than the actual issue.

As a wise 14-year-old puts it, 'I don't think parents should shout at you when they're trying to show their disapproval. But I don't think silence is very good either. When trying to show their feelings they should try to explain them to you without shouting. I think that gets everyone uptight and doesn't solve the problem.'

She's right. But it's so difficult to learn how to begin to hand over, and then relinquish by stages, the control that parents are rightly expected to accept for their children.

Much of the tension-induced shouting would lessen if we could learn to replace some rules by mutually agreed pacts, with responsibility being rewarded by further privileges.

This calls for love, trust, understanding and confidence. But the first step is to recall what effect being shouted at had on us as a child – and still has.

Cut it down when you can, and then it will be all the more effective on the rare occasions when real righteous anger has its place.

PREPARING CHILDREN AT HOME FOR THE ABSENCE OF ONE OF THE FAMILY

Many of us remember being homesick at some time in our lives, and can recapture the panic of trying to control the urge to dash home, especially as night approached. Imagine what it must be like at an age when out of sight is no longer out of mind, but when there is no certainty that those out of sight will ever return. A night feels like forever.

Most of these separations occur when the mother goes into hospital to have a baby, the father goes away on business, or one of the family goes to stay with someone else.

It is difficult to predict how children will react, and one mother was particularly surprised. Ted, a two-year-old, was the youngest of four, and he was so used to people coming and going that he confidently went off with his small suitcase for the odd night with relatives or friends. Then, for the first time, it was his mother who went away for a weekend – and Ted was distressed. Two of the landmarks of his day disappeared. His mother wasn't there to tuck him up in his own bed and kiss him goodnight, and when he went along for his morning cuddle there was only one body in the parental bed.

He went off his food and moped for two days, then clung to her like a limpet for the first few days after her return. It might have helped if she had given him her nightie to take to bed while she was away. Like young animals, children can often smell their mothers even when no one else can, and her presence might have seemed closer, but only if she had worn the nightie for a night or two.

If you, or a brother or sister, have to go into hospital they need to know why. They also need information about hospitals geared to their own understanding; for example a lot of people are in one big bedroom (called a ward), so the doctors and nurses can look after them more easily than by driving cars to all their houses. It may also help to make the link with garages: some jobs on a car can be done at home, but sometimes special things are needed, and the car has to be taken to a garage, where everything that is needed is ready and waiting.

The local Children's Library can provide simple story books about children going to hospital, and these all help to set the scene. So does a walk past the local hospital, on a dry and pleasant day, for visual impact and the memories associated with it are very strong.

Well in advance of the estimated time of departure begin to pack the suitcase together. Leave it open and where it can be seen, and add things slowly so that the eventual separation doesn't come as a shock.

If your child is the one who stays at home, then pack a second small case with a clean handkerchief for every day you expect to be away. His or her responsible job is to give one daily to whoever is left in your place, on the understanding that when they are all gone you will be back to wash some more. If your stay has to be extended, then the situation must be explained, and the child needs to put the extra hankies into the case to reinforce the understanding.

If the visit is to a hospital, then daily visits by the child or children can be valuable in building up an understanding of where you are and what is going on. But the judge of this must be those who know the atmosphere prevailing at the time – if the visit is not for the new baby, then much will depend on the cheerfulness of the ward, and the ability of the patient to be reassuring.

If the separation is for work or a holiday, then you don't need anyone to tell you that a plentiful supply of postcards helps to bridge the gap. But it also helps if the younger children left behind can do something practical as a reminder that the reunion is coming – such as make buns and biscuits to store for a special tea when the waiting is over.

Once the missing member of the family returns he or she may well find a small clinging limpet, literally holding on for several days – but once back the fear of a possible repeat performance looms large for a while.

UNDERSTANDING TEMPER TANTRUMS

As crime and violence escalate around us parents grow more and more concerned both to protect their children from it, and curb their natural tendency towards it. Sometimes circumstances are weighted so heavily against them that they are defeated, and sometimes they over-react to the point where children become unable to stand up for themselves.

We all try to strike the right balance in controlling our children and ourselves. If our own self-control is too rigid it can lead to our nervous exhaustion, and the standard set may be so high that our children feel guilty about their own anger. And if the threshold of our self-control is too low children may become inhibited or hardened. Parents can't win! But it helps to distinguish between temper tantrums, a general tendency towards aggression, and righteous anger.

Some children are naturally placid and easy to bring up. Others are much more difficult, and it isn't the parents' 'fault' – temperamentally they just *are* that way. Both types have the same instincts but the slow ones respond more slowly, and the quick ones more quickly, to the circumstances which lead to frustration.

Apart from obvious reasons, like being over-tired, over-excited or sickening for something, there are two major causes of temper tantrums. One often lies in our mismanagement, but the chief one is that they are a perfectly natural part of a child's development.

One of the greatest skills in child management is timing. Children react badly to being interrupted without warning, and being expected to switch-off their own lives and plug in to ours with instant goodwill. Occasionally it may be necessary, but often it is a thoughtless discourtesy on our part. We haven't seen them as people deeply absorbed in doing something that matters to them, we have only seen them as part of our plan for doing something else that matters to us. How would we like it if – having arranged towels on the beach, anointed ourselves with sun oil, found our dark glasses and our book, and stretched out to bask in the sun – an authoritarian giant said, 'We're going to find a shady spot for a picnic . . . come along . . . quickly . . . hurry up'? We should probably say, 'I'd rather stay here, I'm not hungry yet.' And if they persisted, wouldn't we resist? First to protect our enjoyment in what we were doing, and then out of desire to hit back.

So it is with children. Whatever they are doing is important to them at that moment, and they need at least ten minutes warning when a change of plan lies ahead. Not just time to finish what they are *doing*, but time to emerge from their own world and adjust to entering ours. If they are not given that time, then temper is nature's way of getting rid of strong feelings that can neither be contained nor released in any other way.

The 'terrible twos' is the stage of development when children say to their parents in effect, 'Thank you for loving and caring for me as you have done since I was born. You've built up in me such trust and confidence that I'm ready to be an independent person.'

It is a (difficult) compliment to your upbringing so far.

In establishing independence children need to do things for themselves and, inevitably, to defy those who have been the guiding and ruling force in their lives. Temper tantrums are a healthy sign of development, and we need to respond to this new stage.

Praise children's *efforts* as well as their successes; save-face and reassure them when accidents happen; give them responsible jobs (scrubbing potatoes, filling sandwiches); avoid provoking a crisis, saying No as little as possible, but when you do, stick to it. It is in the face of an absolute No that the pressure of frustration usually bursts from them like a cork from a bottle.

When the showdown comes just let it run its natural course; either leave the child where he or she is while you remove yourself, or remove the child to a quiet room – but don't shut the door. What you need to convey is that you love the child (even though liking isn't part of love at that moment), and that the way back to you is open, but that you don't like, and won't allow, whatever it was that caused the outburst. Eventually the screams will turn to sobs, or sleep, and then you need to be calmly and reassuringly at hand when it is all over; not with lectures but with a friendly welcome which conveys that it's all over.

After that, the pattern varies. Some go back to the starting point and replay the events appropriately (they clear up, or get undressed, or whatever it was that was wanted); others steer clear of the spot where it happened for the rest of the day; some go off quietly to play alone; and some cling like a shadow for the rest of the day, or longer. Just play it by ear. It is a difficult lesson for parents to convey, and children to learn, that it is possible to love the sinner but not the sin.

LOVING THE SINNER, IF NOT THE SIN

The most arresting programme I ever remember seeing on television was a play called, 'Blue Remembered Hills.' Newspapers previewing the event told us it was about a group of children playing in the woods and fields away from parents and habitation, and that the children would all be played by adults. The reasons given for the casting were twofold; it was felt that children couldn't be totally unselfconscious under the eyes of the cameras and crew, but also that children shouldn't be asked to do deliberately what can actually happen in the heat of the moment.

The sight of Colin Welland in schoolboy shorts gallumphing about in the bracken took a bit of getting used to, for about three minutes. And then 'he' disappeared, as did Helen Mirren and the rest of them, and the magic began to work. It was we who were shouting, running, laughing, squabbling and taking-sides, taunting, daring, conspiring and confiding; bundling our dolls into an old pram and dragging and bumping it over tough grassy hillocks; standing on our heads for a dare, being rough, and tender – and free. And sexless. We viewers were part of everyone and everything that happened so carelessly and spontaneously, once these 'children' were away from the constraints of adults and their world of values.

During the play there was a sequence where the children were whooping through the woods on a glorious day, just crashing about with the sheer joy of living and the release of energy that has found an outlet. They began throwing stones, just as part of the spur-of-the-moment purposeless play that is at the very heart of childhood. Then they saw a squirrel way above them, leaping with speed and agility from branch to branch, and it became the target for their throwing. Up went the stones with joyous abandon from below, thrown thoughtlessly by individuals who were enjoying being one of a group more than anything else.

And then the unbelievable happened. A stone found its mark, and the squirrel fell dead at their feet. They were shattered. They froze in their tracks, one turned away to be sick, the others drew near with guilt and remorse striking right to the heart of them. And then, not able to live with such self-condemnation, they tried to justify their actions: 'Squirrels do a lot of harm to crops . . . they are vermin really . . . some farmers pay a penny a tail for dead squirrels . . . we've done a kind of service in a way . . .'

These children surely spoke to and for all of us. I doubt whether any of us has escaped doing something on the spur of the moment which we recognized almost immediately as being wrong. And then we try to justify ourselves – don't we?

Could it have happened differently for those children? If an adult had been there the incident might not have happened at all, but then, neither might they have benefited from the innocent and life-giving release of physical and emotional energy in the pure play that had gone before. Preventing people from being 'bad' doesn't automatically mean that they are 'good'; it may just mean that they are inhibited.

As parents we must anticipate and accept that children are going to do wrong again and again. If we are too angry and punitive we may drive them to concealment, evasion and self-justification. If we let them get away with it, they may never 'see' the consequences of their actions. If we can understand and, even though we may be angry about what they have *done,* we forgive *them* (certainly before bedtime), then they may learn from their mistakes.

A lovely Irish woman said of her mother recently, 'She used to be furious with us about whatever it was, and say, "How *could* you do that? You knew perfectly well it was wrong." And we used to stand there wanting to die. And then she would reach out to pull us to her, saying "Och, your poor little face . . . come here then . . . what you did was very wrong . . . but, God, how I love you . . . there now, let's make a pot of tea and have a nice time together."'

DEAD OR ALIVE?

One of the many difficulties children have is in distinguishing between alive, dead and inanimate.

The 'living' category is the easy one. Right from their earliest awareness the people who love and care for them are life itself. People move, talk, laugh, eat, feel warm to the touch, can do all manner of things, and interact physically and emotionally; they are very much alive.

So are cats and dogs. They move, purr, bark, eat, are warm, can come and go and sleep, and respond in a relationship.

Fish can't be taken out of their tank to be touched, but the fact that they move constantly, and have to be fed and looked after, puts them in the 'live' category, too.

Then comes death, cold and still, followed by disappearance. The word 'dead' needs to be used in a perfectly ordinary voice, with no emotion, on every possible occasion.

A dead bird, butterfly or fish is one that used to be alive, but now isn't alive any longer. Children usually want to inspect it, for it is so much easier to examine something that is motionless. They look at herrings before we cook them, so why are we so squeamish about putting the dead goldfish on kitchen paper if they want to have a look? Our attitude to death is very important to children. Meanwhile, we must be quietly matter of fact, neither callous nor sentimental, neither squeamish nor ghoulish; for children need to accept the fact of 'dead' before it happens to a person or pet with whom they are emotionally involved.

Plants are alive, and they die. They need water (through which they also get their food), warmth and light. They 'move' upwards and sideways, and downwards (especially if they are carrots) but they can't run about. They grow, produce flowers, the flowers die, the seeds ripen and drop, and more flowers grow from the tiny seeds. Young children don't need detailed explanations (that can come much later), but they do need us to 'throw away the dead flowers', and to 'save seeds' from plants such as beans and nasturtiums in order that they can be sown next year to make new plants. Very slowly they become aware of all these connections, and when eventually they learn about 'the life cycle' at school they will have a crowd of memories that surge up and come together to give real understanding.

The inanimate category includes things like stones, nails, gumboots and lamp-posts. They don't eat, sleep or move, and they haven't got feelings. So far, so good. But what about wooden tables? They are inanimate now, but once they were living, 'eating', breathing trees. And we sometimes add to the confusion by saying to a child who has bumped into the table, 'Naughty table to hurt you, let's give it a smack', as though it was alive.

There are other confusions. A washing machine moves and makes a noise; a car 'goes' if it is fed with petrol and turned-on; 'home' is very much alive, but some of us who have been house hunting will have felt empty houses to be warm and friendly, or blankly impersonal, or even chilling to the point of fear.

Children also have another classification all their own; inanimate objects which they invest with life. That object is carried around, talked to, put to bed, scolded and loved. Go along with this, for in their imaginations it has feelings, it is human – it is them.

ACCEPTING HELP THAT HINDERS

There are givers and takers in life, but not all givers are gracious enough to receive when others try to do some of the giving. Children need help to learn how to do both, but they can't if parents – out of love or hurry – insist on doing everything for them.

It isn't easy to be patient when so much of the early 'helping' goes wrong, but it is disheartening for children to be scolded for mishaps without even being thanked for their good intentions.

It is easier to be patient when we understand what is happening, and this is particularly true of spills of one sort or another. You know the scene: your child has watched you pour milk countless times, and one day says 'Jimmy do it!' You hand over the jug, the pouring commences with great care, you say 'Stop!' but the pouring continues and the milk overflows.

Why wasn't your 'Stop!' obeyed? It was, but the warning probably came too late to make allowance for a still immature nervous system.

Nerves are minute bundles of threads which pass messages to each other, from all over the body to the brain. The brain processes the message, and sends the answer back down the nerve bundles to the appropriate part of the body for action. Two ears fed your 'Stop!' into the nervous system, which carried the message to the brain, which sent the 'stop pouring' message back along the nerves of the arm to the wrist, but not instantaneously as it does with us. By the time the message arrived the damage was done, and you were both distressed.

Find a mug with a bold distinguishing mark about 2 in. from the bottom, and offer a half-pint jug only half full of milk. A big jug is too heavy; and a full jug, even a small one, pours the liquid out so quickly that the child has no time to assess where the lip of the jug is in relation to the rim of the mug. We forget that we once had to learn these skills.

Then say to the child, 'Pour the milk just up to the top of the red line . . .', and as he pours very slowly and carefully the chances are that at, or about, the red line his eyes will send the 'Stop!' message to his brain, and by the time the message to stop pouring comes back, and the jug is tipped upright, the milk will probably be half way between the red line and the top of the mug. But at least it won't have overflowed, unless, that is, his eye was deflected from the milk in the mug to the red line on the outside, with the consequent moving of the wrist to the left or right (according to which way his head tilted to see the line).

Once we understand how much there is to learn for children who are meeting everyday challenges for the first time in their lives, then it is much easier to greet the inevitable spill or two with the magic words, 'It's all right . . .' as we go for the cloth.

HELPING CHILDREN TO MAKE CONNECTIONS

The morning of George's second birthday was a great success. The postman delivered a stack of cards and parcels, and George sat on the floor and dealt purposefully with the opening of the envelopes. Some flaps had just been tucked in, some were stuck at the centre but left room for fingers to wriggle and tear their way inside, and some were so impenetrable that a little help was needed to protect the contents from damage. Opening each envelope was such an absorbing challenge that the cards were a bit of an anti-climax – they were tossed aside while the next envelope was tackled. But when they were all opened, then the cards received minute attention, especially those with 'I am 2' badges. Then came the scrutiny of the pictures, with animals and objects being identified and his mother being required to 'read' them to him, by which he meant 'tell me about the picture'.

All this time the parcels had been ignored, for he didn't really know much about parcels. But once started, the undoing for its own sake was more important and satisfying than the contents. Only when all the undoing was over did he turn his attention to the presents, inspecting and experimenting briefly with each, before exhaustion suddenly overcame him and he had to be put to bed for a nap. He woke refreshed, had lunch, and then said confidently, 'More parcels . . .' His mother explained that there weren't any more. He looked baffled, then a possible connection dawned, and he snuggled up to her saying, '*Please* Mummy, more parcels . . .?' She again explained, and went through the presents telling him who had sent each one, and saying that the postman had brought them all safely to him, but that there weren't any more. He had listened intently and appeared to accept it, until another connection registered somewhere in his mind. His face lit up as he said with certainty, 'Mummy *buy* more parcels!' All that mental effort, and still it couldn't produce another parcel, so he gave up, and turned his attention to the presents themselves.

Christmas came, and card-opening was shared, with George keeping his own cards on a shelf where he could reach them. The parcels under the tree were given out to everyone on Christmas Day, and were enjoyed to the full. No more were requested.

Some months elapsed, and George was invited to a party. Thomas's birthday was talked about, and a small present was carefully chosen by George on a shopping expedition which didn't have to be hurried. He also chose some paper, and helped to wrap up the present. So far, so good. He duly handed over the parcel on arrival, and set about removing his anorak. When he entered the party room and saw Thomas on the floor surrounded by parcels, the visual image clicked into his mental computer and came up with the answer: he knew *exactly* what you had to do with a pile of birthday parcels!

His mother intervened, and with explanations gently removed a parcel from his clutches. He accepted the interference reluctantly, and was unexpectedly rewarded by Thomas giving him a parcel to open. George brightened and set about the task enthusiastically, but was then devastated when Thomas wanted the actual present. It was too much to bear, he clutched it fiercely, saying 'Mine, mine . . .', and burst into tears.

None of this will be new to you, but we must never lose sight of just how much children have to learn in the first two years of their lives – more than they will ever again learn in any other two-year period. It isn't only the learning of skills like walking, feeding themselves, dressing, opening envelopes and manipulating objects. They also have to learn a foreign language, both to understand what is said, and to make themselves known, and everything has its own name, and sometimes several names (jersey, jumper, woolly). The really intricate bit is making the connections between the various bits of knowledge that are slowly being absorbed.

Poor George was struggling with post offices, pillar-boxes, postmen, letters and parcels; absent friends and relations, who could give him things without being there; post-parcels and shopping-parcels; the magic word Please (which sometimes fails), and the meaning of yours, mine, ours, his, hers and theirs. He had made so many connections, but suddenly intellect cut-out and emotions took over.

Our children's effort to learn is constant, demanding and complex beyond our imagination; their safeguard is our love, and nature's insistence that they cry or rage when the pressure becomes intolerable.

AVOIDING HURTFUL COMPARISONS

The other day I was dressing after a swim when I became aware of a family in the next cubicle. There was a flop as something went down on the floor, and the corner of a baby's changing mat slid into view. Then came a warm and loving voice saying, 'Who's a clever boy, then? And what will Daddy say when we get home? We'll tell him "Daddy we've been swimming, and you've got one big boy and one who's a sissy – and guess which is which?" And won't he be surprised?'

I finished dressing and pulled back the curtain, and there they all were. A young mother kneeling on the floor powdering a beautiful baby who was cooing and kicking. And an equally beautiful toddler, warmly wrapped in a large white bath towel sitting on the bench waiting for his turn.

I stopped to talk, and naturally she was excited that, at their first visit to the baths, the baby had taken to it like a duckling to water. Then she smiled warmly at the toddler, and said, 'But you didn't like it, did you? You didn't want to go in. You were a sissy!'

Because she so clearly adored them both I risked saying to the older one, 'I'm on your side, it's cold and splashy and too big, isn't it? It's easy for babies because they don't know what it's all about.' I don't suppose he understood a word, but his mother said at once, 'Well, yes, it is big isn't it? He loved it in the summer when I put a bath out in the garden – he was in and out all the time.'

We chatted for a bit and then, looking at the baby, she said, 'I suppose he could go off it later on, if something happens to frighten him?' Indeed he could – just as the 22-month-old could learn to love the water again once he has adjusted to the size, sound and smell of this large and unfamiliar building.

I wondered how she came to use the word 'sissy'; it certainly wasn't intended as a taunt. It was almost as though her associations with the word were happy ones. I could imagine her playing with school friends, and someone calling out, 'Come on, race you to the steps – last one home's a sissy!'

So her use of the word didn't matter too much perhaps, except that when he grows older he may hear it from others in a different context. And then the old myth could be perpetrated whereby we come to feel that it is shameful to be apprehensive in the face of a new experience. It is *natural* to feel apprehension; it is nature's way both of protecting us, and gearing us up to 'go' if proper caution doesn't tell us to 'stop'.

Children need time and support in the face of new experiences. We all do, in order that we can come to recognize, and accept, the perfectly natural 'butterflies' that will always be part of our lives, if we have the courage to go on doing new things.

What mattered more was the look of deflation on the little fellow's face. He felt excluded from the approving relationship between his mother and the baby; he knew that he hadn't met with the same approval. It is hurtful to feel 'unloved', especially over something that isn't your fault. Yet think of the number of times we all put children in this position, not because we don't love and respect them but because we are thoughtless. We meet a friend, and looking at our toddler admiringly she says, 'Isn't he a lovely boy, aren't you lucky, I wish I had one like that', and before he can bask in the compliment we say, 'Oh! He's a little pest. You can have him anytime!' Why couldn't the response be, 'Yes, aren't we lucky'?

Children have a sense of fun, but not our adult sense of humour. They take things literally, and must find us hurtful or bewildering if not worrying more often than we realize. Later on they will probably find us embarrassing or irritating!

Which of us hasn't known what it feels like to go out of our way to prepare a specially nice meal for friends or relations, only to hear the time-honoured 'joke', 'I'm glad you've come, we only get properly fed when there are visitors?'

God forbid we should lose our sense of humour, but sometimes graceful acceptance, or a compliment, doesn't come amiss. At any age.

TRACING THE ORIGIN OF SOME OF THE GUILT IN PARENTHOOD

Why do so many people, particularly mothers, feel endlessly guilty about almost everything? Whenever anything goes wrong they automatically think it is their fault, and feel that they should have been able to avoid it happening.

This state of affairs has reached such epidemic proportions that in talking about it one day to about 200 mothers I asked how many of them were free of this crippling, and usually unnecessary, feeling. Only one hand went up, and when I said, 'Thank goodness there is at least one of you,' she replied, 'Well, there isn't actually because I feel guilty about not feeling guilty!'

On another occasion I asked a group if anyone could give an example of the sort of irrational things that made them feel guilty, and one said immediately, 'I can. Just when we were going to bed last night my husband said, "The radiator cap in the hall is cracked" – and I felt guilty.' She went on to say that she knew it wasn't her fault, it had nothing to do with her, she wasn't even aware of it, but she still felt guilty.

I said, 'Suppose the word "guilt" had never been invented, what word would you have used instead to describe what you felt?', and immediately she said, 'Fear.' Wilfully misunderstanding her I continued, 'But even if the radiator had leaked it would only have been water, not sulphuric acid. And even if the water had gushed out and soaked the carpets and made an awful mess, it wouldn't have trapped and drowned you all. So what were you afraid of?' Back came the immediate reply, 'My husband.' Clearly this could have been a rational possibility, but she went on, 'And that's silly, because he's never even been impatient with me, let alone angry, ever since I've known him.' I asked if 'fear' was still the right word, and if it wasn't then what was? She agreed that it wasn't, but thought for some time before she said, 'I don't know quite, I suppose it is "inadequate" or something like that.' Then she traced these feelings right back to childhood. She had had a happy home, and loved her parents, but the picture that emerged was of a mother who was busy, capable and a bit impatient. The first childlike efforts to tie shoe laces, scrub vegetables, make paper chains, learn to knit, and to do all the hundreds of things that have to be tackled for the first time, met with impatience.

There was a kindly but constant refrain of, 'Not like that, like this,' 'Here, let me do it,' 'Now look what you've done!' 'Run off and play, it's quicker to do it myself.' She just grew up feeling that she wasn't quick enough, clever enough or good enough to measure up to her parents' standards of efficient capability.

She has spent her whole life doing her best, but with so little confidence in herself that whenever anything went wrong she automatically felt it must somehow be due to the fact that she 'wasn't good enough' to keep everything running perfectly.

This is the way life has been for countless others. If we grow up with a low self-esteem then we never discover or quite believe the strengths and gifts we all have within us. And if we don't break out of the depressing pattern that conditioned us, we are almost bound to pass it on to our children. If we see what happened, and consciously try to correct it, then we can say to our children when they begin to learn, 'Well done, you've nearly got it,' 'Never mind, we can soon mop it up,' 'Don't worry, it's difficult now but one day you will be able to do it.' And then they won't have to inherit our burden.

Don't imagine I am trying to get rid of guilt altogether – that would be dangerously shortsighted. But if we could rid ourselves of endless false guilt, then we might be better able to accept, and do something about, those feelings of genuine guilt which tell us we have missed the mark.

MODERN FATHERHOOD

Fortunately there are more than enough men who have taken to full fatherhood like ducks to water for it to be certain that the trend will continue. But that doesn't mean that every expectant mother should be equally expectant that her mate will become an instant and enthusiastically involved father from pre-natal classes onwards via the delivery room.

It was time for fathers to be given free access to the previously enclosed emotional world of mothers and children, for everyone's sake. Yet it goes against the grain for some couples and has come too suddenly for others.

This was brought home to me by people's reactions to a tragic court case in the papers. A child had been taken to hospital with horrific injuries, including brain damage which would leave the child blind and mentally retarded for life. And it was brought about by the mother's jealousy.

As I remember it a young mother had given birth to her first baby with her husband in attendance. They were both over the moon, but then he had to return to his ship in the Merchant Navy. She had to care for the baby alone, and was particularly nervous and lacking in confidence. Each time her husband came home he enthusiastically took-over the baby, doing everything for her, never seeing that his wife felt excluded, inadequate and relegated to second best compared with his nautical efficiency in everything he did. The last straw came when he pushed his daughter to the clinic with her, and insisted on undressing the baby and putting her on the scales: 'He showed me up in front of all the other mothers, and made me look a fool.'

For the next few days everyone was talking about it in shops and bus queues: 'She should have been glad of his help, mine never lifted a finger,' 'What a wicked thing to do, there's no excuse,' 'Typical! Doing what he wanted to do, without any thought for his wife,' 'She's welcome to a husband as sissy as that, but she shouldn't have hurt the baby,' 'What did a lovely man like that want to marry her for?'

The one comment I never heard was, 'I wonder how many of us made our *men* feel shut-out, foolish and inadequate when we were young mothers?' I'm afraid a lot of us did, and still do. Many men have more than enough difficulties to overcome without their partners undermining their new willingness to be physically and emotionally involved with their children.

Some men learned from their own parents that it didn't pay to show fear, grief or tenderness – it wasn't manly. And after a lifetime of learning to repress these deep emotions it is hard to change. But if they can share in the birth they are almost always moved so deeply that the taboo on feelings is broken, and they are set free to start learning to feel and live freely again. But others can't yet face the intimacy of birth, partly because they feel squeamish about pain and blood, or because they feel afraid that they might not live up to what they feel is expected of them, or because their formative years still leave them feeling that it somehow isn't quite right to witness any sort of bodily evacuation.

Other men have always known they were the apple of their mother's eye, and take it for granted that they will be the centre of their partner's life as well. When it comes to fatherhood some find it easy to share that central place with their own child, but some don't; they feel that love given to the baby is taken away from them.

Some men channel all their creativity into their work, and are content to let the baby be largely the mother's personal creation.

Others lack confidence in general, and feel under constant pressure to prove themselves both at work and at home, and being asked to prove themselves at fatherhood as well is just too much. So they relegate themselves to a back seat, supporting the mother in every way, but leaving all the decisions to her.

When it comes to parenthood there are no oughts and musts and shoulds – only what is possible given the past and the present circumstances. But we don't have to be prisoners of our past. In order to learn, opportunities have to be offered, recognized, and taken up. And if fatherhood is taken up, then it needs to be encouraged with mutual generosity, and good will.

POSITION IN THE FAMILY

Over the years we have all grown accustomed to people telling us that the eldest children in a family are always highly strung because they are the guinea pigs . . . that middle children are always difficult . . . that the baby is always spoilt . . . that the fourth and subsequent ones are no trouble because they bring each other up . . . and that only children are lonely and selfish.

Sweeping generalizations like these have a certain amount of truth in them, otherwise they wouldn't have stayed in circulation. Yet I sometimes think we invite problems for ourselves and our children by making these assumptions about their position in the family; or do we fall back gratefully on these clichés as an explanation and excuse for what we would otherwise see as our mistakes?

Every child is an individual, and right from the moment of conception the chromosomes determine the genetic make-up of each one, the baby is already going to be a boy or a girl, tall or short, who will have blue or brown eyes, and a tendency to inherit certain other traits from one side of the family or another. Some babies are easy, placid and have a sunny temperament right from birth. Some are restless, cry a lot, and take weeks or even months to settle down. It is a matter of sheer chance which type of baby arrives first.

And this is true of every baby in the family – there is an element of chance which pre-determines, up to a point, what type of child he or she will be. Whatever the position in the family.

There is also another natural factor common to children in any family: there will be rivalry. No matter how careful we are to be fair in everything, and no matter how uncompetitive we may be ourselves, and no matter how careful we are to convey to the children that we love them for what they are rather than what they can do, there will still be rivalry. At times it will exhibit itself in fighting and squabbling; at other times one or another will revert to baby behaviour, to try to get attention that way; or to the pursuit of excellence in one chosen sphere; or to telling tales, to 'down' the other in order to 'up' themselves; their jealousy may surface as spite.

All these behaviour patterns have far less to do with chronological position in the family than to the needs of any person in a group, the need to be loved and valued, the need to contribute in order to feel a sense of satisfaction and worth, the need to feel that adults are fair.

If we consider these needs, then we can more easily see how age affects the way in which they may be met. Teenagers often go through a stage of not wanting to be kissed or touched in any way, but they will know they are loved if they are trusted. The 'baby' of 6 or more still needs demonstrative affection, and the teenagers may delight in showing it to this member of the family when they can't stand it from anyone else. This is fine, as long as the 'baby' isn't allowed to overstep the limits that each of us should set in our relationships. And the 'baby' needs to be put in positions of responsibility in order to receive praise and gratitude for services rendered, as well as kisses for being cuddly.

The greatest difficulty of all for parents is the struggle to be fair to each child, in the eyes of each child. It's a game we can't win! But we can go on trying.

It isn't 'fair' that the younger ones can't go to a party, but it is perfectly fair that the party-givers shall invite only those they want. It isn't 'fair' that older members of the family have more pocket money, but they have more experience of handling money and are therefore given an increasing amount with which to budget. It isn't 'fair' that babies have so much of their mother's time, but every baby has to be taken care of at the helpless stage.

In all these, and countless other, instances children are wanting equality rather than fairness, and we need to help them to understand the difference. We must also help them to experience and enjoy the lovely compensations belonging to each age and stage, and to be as aware of them as they are of the admitted limitations of those same stages.

We may not see these deeper fundamental issues if we just put difficulties down to the popular explanation of position in the family.

FAVOURITISM IN THE FAMILY

If you love one of your children more than the others, stop feeling guilty about it; if that's the way it is, face it. Then, paradoxically, you may find that you are free to understand a great deal that you hadn't seen before which may help you to resolve the situation.

Almost all parents have a last minute panic before their second child is born, and feel that it wouldn't be possible to love another baby as much as they love the one they already have. This doubt may even survive for a time after the second birth, and it isn't unusual for parents to remember the earlier birth and say ruefully, 'I'd forgotten how ugly newborn babies can be!'

But the very act of caring for someone can create the bond of love. The panic subsides, and each child creates its own special place in the family. Once this is discovered then subsequent pregnancies and births are usually free of this particular fear.

Occasionally there are exceptions to this, and under certain circumstances a parent may conceive a positive hatred of a baby at birth or soon after. If this happens skilled professional advice and help are essential. It is nothing to be ashamed of, or guilty about, it is simply a sign that something is wrong and needs to be resolved. If this happens to you in hospital, then tell the sister in charge of your ward: if you have left the hospital, then go to your doctor and make sure he or she understands the depth of your feelings. If you are in such a state that you can do neither, then contact Parents Anonymous (see *Useful Addresses*) and talk to someone who has been through it all before you.

But this isn't the favouritism, or active dislike which concerns parents who love all their children, but have a specially soft spot for one. It may be for the child who is most like them, because they understand what is going on inside the child and can identify so readily; on the other hand, recognizing the characteristics that give us most trouble in our own lives can cause a clash of temperaments.

Sometimes the favoured one is the easiest; if parents are afraid of aggression then they may feel safest with the one who won't threaten their self-control, or their control over him or her.

Quite often the reverse is true, and it is the one who is always up to mischief and in trouble who endears him or herself in a special way, especially if the parents are confident and outgoing people who don't panic too much, and can enjoy their sturdy individualist.

The favourite may be exactly like a young edition of the partner they married, or very like a dearly loved parent of their own – seeing history repeat itself can be fascinating and endearing.

Some children have charm in abundance, and keep it all their lives; some have a vulnerability that also stays as an integral part of their personality; some are gloriously larger than life; some are solidly reliable from the beginning.

Each child is a *person*, and we can't love all persons 'the same' because each is different. Perhaps this is what causes the anxiety, the difference between 'the same' and 'as much as'. I have yet to meet the parents who wouldn't give their lives to save any one of their children, and you can't love more than that.

What we can, and must, do is to be fair in the children's eyes. If the big one isn't allowed to take toys away from the little one, then the little one mustn't be allowed to take toys away from the big one. Either they have treats simultaneously, or each has a specially chosen treat. Either we make allowances for all, or none (unless there is an explained reason). If one has pocket money at a certain age, then the others should receive it at the same age (though the amounts may differ according to age). If they enjoy hugs and kisses, then each needs their fill. All must be praised, thanked, and valued, for what they are and try to do, not according to their looks or ability.

Mark you, even if you are as fair and wise as Solomon, each of your children is still almost bound to feel that 'the other one' is the favourite! When we look back to our own parents we can cease to think in terms of one or other being 'the favourite' and understand that there was, and is, a natural affinity between some children and parents – and that is a very different thing from favouritism.

DISTINGUISHING BETWEEN LOVE AND INDULGENCE

On a spring holiday my husband and I witnessed an episode that has stayed in our minds. As it may provide as much food for thought for you as it did for us, I would like to share it.

Our walk had brought us to an ancient walled city, and we were lingering over coffee in the sunny forecourt of a small taverna. We were joined by a tall genial father, a happy loving mother, a son of about 13 and a daughter of about 11.

The father said, 'What do you all want?' whereupon the mother said, 'I'd just like a coffee, please', and the children said in unison, 'Ice-cream!' We weren't aware of them after that until the father said, 'I say, here they come . . . what about *that* for ice-creams?' And the children's eyes lit up as they beheld two large glass bowls filled with generous scoops of chocolate, vanilla, strawberry and almond ice-cream, topped by fresh strawberries and whipped cream, and decorated with little paper parasols. Without more ado the children set to. The parents enjoyed their delight and looked on smiling.

Then the father said to his daughter, 'Can you spare me a taste of your cream? She shook her head and ploughed on. When she was halfway through her mother said, 'Couldn't you spare Daddy some now?' Again there was an unsmiling shake of the head, and the dish was emptied with every indication of satisfaction, but not a word or gesture to express her pleasure.

I found myself hoping that when the father went to pay the bill the mother would say with quiet authority, 'Your father has worked a whole year to afford this holiday for us all, and you can't even give him a spoonful of ice-cream. This won't do. If he is generous enough to offer you another of these very expensive treats, then you must offer him the first, biggest and best mouthful without waiting to be asked.'

Later we found ourselves on the same guided tour of the castle, the daughter moping and leaning on her mother, who put an arm round her saying, 'It won't be long now, and then we'll do what you want to do.' And this time I found myself hoping that the father would find a quiet moment to say with the same kindly authority, 'Don't spoil things for your mother. If you're bored you can both go back to the entrance and wait for us on the steps – but don't leave the steps.'

It is pointless to say to children, 'When I was your age we didn't even have holidays, let alone holidays abroad . . .', and it smacks of martyrdom if parents defend themselves in a self-pitying way. But if parents don't speak up for each other, how are children to learn to be less self-centred?

Ironically, children like this usually grow up to be equally loving (or indulgent?) uncomplaining parents themselves. From birth onwards they are absorbing memories of 'this is what parents do, this is how they behave', and when it is their turn these same patterns tend to come to the surface to be repeated.

The difficulties come in the years between. Self-centred youngsters go into jobs (if they can get them) with the idea that they are going to be paid to do what they want to do, and when it doesn't all go their way there are moans of 'it isn't fair that . . .', and 'I don't see why . . .'

If parents are either endlessly self-centred, or self-giving, then children lack a pattern for this next stage of their lives.

HELPING CHILDREN TO UNDERSTAND MONEY

When we talk about someone handling money well we mean they budget wisely. If we say money just slips through their fingers we mean it is spent without care or planning. What we often overlook is that in the early stages of learning about money children need to handle it physically.

Try building up a selection of coins, at least two of everything but preferably more. Scrub, Dettol, rinse and dry them, and keep them in a special purse to be played with – the early play stages having nothing to do with playing shops, but everything to do with handling money.

Get out the purse one day, put it on the table and say, 'Look what's in there?' – and let the child do just that. Sit nearby, mostly for safety because small coins can be swallowed or pushed into noses or ears, but also to see unobtrusively that the money stays on the table. Even at this stage the idea needs to be conveyed that money is important and has to be looked after carefully.

The first stages of this learning play are likely to be the spreading of the coins about with the palm of the hand, or picking them up until no more can be held. Just let the exploration continue without comment; it takes a lot of handling to become familiar with the look, feel and weight of money – probably day after day if it is enjoyed.

When interest eventually wanes try pointing to one coin and ask if there are any more like it. Interest may be roused, and identical coins put together.

Another time point out the crowned head on a coin, and ask who it is and if there are any more like it. Eventually the reverse sides may be looked at with interest, and sorted out according to the emblems or the number on them.

After several or many such play periods they may enjoy the game of 'Can you find me a penny? A 2-penny piece? A 10-penny piece?' And later on the game of swopping one coin for others of a similar value. But let each stage come and go in the child's own time and way; let it all be *play* at this stage.

Until coins are familiar children are not really ready to understand buying – which is the exchange of coins for goods.

No one can tell you when to start pocket money, or how much it should be. This is a family decision based on memories, and updated by careful thought and discussions with others in a similar position. But whatever you decide there are certain factors that are constant. Whether you start at 3, 5 or 7 years, and whether the amount is 5 or 50 pence, some children will always have a few pennies left over at the end of the week, and others will always have spent the lot within an hour of receiving it.

Be patient about this, and accept that young children spend according to their temperament. It doesn't follow that thrifty children will prosper financially, or that they will be so cautious about everything that they can never throw the occasional cap over the windmill. And the spendthrift one isn't destined to be perpetually penniless, or in debt. Children's temperaments remain different, but their judgement matures.

Look on pocket money as a faithfully regular gift, with no strings attached. Children should be able to trust you on this, to the very day. If you withhold it, or part of it, as a punishment or for damages, far from teaching them the value of money it is more likely to be seen as a breach of faith on your part at this stage.

Neither can a young child be expected to understand little lectures on 'wasting money', or 'it took a lot of hard work to earn that money', for the very simple reason that 'hard work' to a child is play at its most glorious and satisfying! And 'What's so hard about that?' they might say, if only it wasn't beyond them to make such connections consciously, and express them.

Real learning is a very slow process. In the early years be content to support children while they become familiar with the fundamentals of spending money. What will it buy? How many alternatives are there? Why can't you get it back? How do you wait a whole week for more? How can you live comfortably with regrets?

Meanwhile, go on helping them to understand money spending in small ways, such as counting out the bus fare from your purse before you go out, being responsible for its safety, stating the destination and buying the tickets, and disposing of them in the proper place at the end of the journey.

HONESTY IS MORE IMPORTANT THAN TACT

Which of us hasn't experienced the awful moment when, at a crowded bus stop, our 4-year-old says loudly, 'Hasn't that man got a fat nose? Has a bee stung it?' If we were brought up not to hurt people's feelings our first thought is probably for the man's distress and embarrassment, and our second thought is for ourselves. What will everybody think of us for having brought up such a rude child? In the heat of the moment we are likely to hear ourselves say, 'Ssh! Look at that big dog over there,' if not 'Ssh! Don't be silly/rude/unkind.'

Why is it that our child so often seems to come last on our list of those whose feelings mustn't be hurt?

But what are we supposed to do? Say 'Yes, it's huge isn't it? But not a bee – more like six pints of beer a day'? Unthinkable! But if we had had prior notice we might have been able to manage, 'No, some people have nice big noses, and some have small ones, but they are all just as good for smelling things. You can smell a lot with yours, can't you? What smells do you like best?' and on we could go following our red herring. Or (and you might be surprised to discover how often this can happen) we could catch the man's eye and find that he is grinning in huge delight, or even ready to join in the conversation.

So often we invest other people with the feelings we think we might have in a similar situation, and half the time they aren't feeling like that at all. Odder still, if only we stopped to put ourselves in that position we would know that we wouldn't mind either. Children are so innocent and trusting, they just speak as they find; it is we who complicate the issue.

And we really do complicate it more than we know.

We want them to be truthful, but if the truth doesn't please us we react sharply. What is a child to do? Go on being honest, and discomforted? Or decide that it isn't worth it, and keep the interesting observations private? But how do you know which observations are going to earn a rebuke if you don't try them out? Better not risk it! Just keep quiet – only after a bit it's easier not to bother to notice things at all. Apathy and lack of interest set in, and the lesson is already being learned that it is safer not to take risks than to lay yourself open to public rebuke.

The same may hold good at school – don't answer in case you are wrong!

But the complication can go deeper than that when we realize how many times we may have denied the truth of our child's intuition, just because it embarrasses us socially, by saying such things as, 'Dont be so silly, of *course* you like Auntie Cissie, come and give her a nice kiss.' If children don't like someone it is for a very good reason according to their instincts or experience, and we should think very carefully indeed before undermining their honest reaction. One day we may want to say 'Don't kiss or be touched by anyone if you don't want to be; follow your instinct,' so where will they be if we have already interfered with their instinct about people?

Better to say, 'I think it's one of those days when you don't like any of us much, so run along and play', but find time afterwards and say, 'Now, tell me about Auntie Cissie . . .' and *listen.* Then agree that in future you won't insist that kisses are given, but ask them to tell you of their reservations privately in future.

TWINS

We have two sets of twins in our family, identical girls, and boys who don't resemble each other more than ordinary brothers.

At school I remember two sets of twins. One pair looked, and were, quite dissimilar in almost every way, and yet they were incredibly close; the others were identical, but I remember being able to tell them apart by looking into their eyes:

one twin looked back confidently, the other's gaze flickered and fell.

Last summer there were pictures in all the papers of identical sisters, married to identical brothers, who had produced babies within an hour of each other – the first recorded happening of its kind as far as was known.

Twins are a fascinating subject, and since they are not all that rare it seemed worthwhile making enquiries of twins, and parents of twins, to see if they have any messages to pass on. And they have.

On looking back to childhood, grown-up twins remember their intense dislike of being referred to as 'the twins', or 'the twinnies'. Even when they were identical they resented the loss of their individuality, and wanted to be called, and referred to, by their own names. They *hated* being asked, 'Which one are you?' At least a sincere, 'Are you Hazel or Ann' indicated that some effort was being made to establish their identity. However, every coin has its reverse side, and the opposite of which-one-are-you was the fun they had in playing tricks on people by deliberately confusing them.

They all remembered the comfort of having each other, whether or not they were identical, especially at night – quite often although they had separate beds they would gravitate to one. Many of them recorded a sense of disappointment if they were given identical presents, as one put it, 'If she opened hers first, there was no point in opening mine – I already knew what was in it.'

The lesson to be learned from this seems to be that if they want different things, then give them just that. But if both want t-shirts, then let them be different; after all they can swap when they want to.

Although they may have wanted to be together and share everything, they didn't like the *assumption* that this would be so. They wanted to feel free to make different friends, and to do different things. Many remembered the pleasure of being taken on special outings, but on different days and to do different things. Apart from feeling individuals in their own right, it also gave them the novel experience of having something different to talk about together.

Remembering all these things some parents start their twins at playgroup together, and then let them branch out by having an extra session each but on different days. This can be particularly helpful if the children are not 'equal' in every way; it simply doesn't follow that their academic ability, their aptitude for dancing, or jig-saw puzzles, or anything else, is identical even in identical twins. It is never fair or kind to compare children in a family with each other, but it is particularly insensitive to make comparisons between twins.

Individuality is as important as similarity, and parents need to encourage (but not 'make') their twins to have a life and mind of their own, as well as their shared lives.

Several twins mentioned the difficulties of marriage, especially if their childhood hadn't encouraged their individuality. Sometimes different husbands, homes and lifestyles were unsettling. Sometimes there was jealousy at having someone come between them. One brother married and had to go abroad on business, leaving his wife with his twin sister who was devastated on picking up the phone one evening to hear him say, 'Is Eileen there?' She found it hard to come second.

One mother, who is herself a twin and the mother of twins, must have spoken for many when she said, 'I try to remember all the things I hated, and to avoid them, but there's no getting away from the fact that twins *are* special. People always notice them wherever we go, and the opening gambit is always, "Are they twins?" or "Twins – how lovely!" and you *do* feel pleased and proud and the centre of attention, and they *do* look lovely dressed alike to accentuate their twinness!' Of course they do, and it is.

As always, it is a question of balance and recognizing the feelings and needs of the twins – not just in childhood but bearing in mind that separations and marriage may lie ahead.

LEFT-HANDEDNESS

I was in a playgroup one day, watching four children at the cutting-out and sticking table. They were having a lovely time, snipping bits of paper, straw, ribbon, rug wool and material into pieces which were then being stuck on paper. A tremendous amount of learning was going on, though the children were at very different stages of mastering the various skills.

One could master both the scissors and the sticking; one could manage the cutting, but the sticking was a real problem – the glue was everywhere, sticking things together that she didn't want stuck at all; the third had switched to experimenting with the sticking, making bigger and bigger 'sandwiches'. And the fourth was battling manfully to make the scissors cut, but they wouldn't.

The child's mother sat beside him, obviously anxious that he couldn't do what the others managed so easily. She positioned his grip on the scissors, took a pair herself, and very patiently tried to teach him, 'Look, like this . . . open them up, open his mouth . . . now shut his mouth on the paper.' The child tried and tried, then grew distressed. His mother grew impatient, and had the good sense to walk away. The child put down the scissors and began to tear and stick instead. I picked up the scissors, used them for a while, and then put them down in front of him but well to the left. A few minutes later he picked them up spontaneously with his left hand, and cut what he wanted to cut with no difficulty at all.

Going over to his mother I said, 'Have you seen your son? He's suddenly got the hang of it. Things usually take a bit longer with left-handers, don't they?' She looked at him with amazement, then said, 'I didn't know he was left-handed!' I asked if anyone else in the family was and she said, 'Yes, his father. Why on earth didn't I think of it?'

She had no need to blame herself. Babies usually use both hands equally easily, and although some children are strongly left-handed from quite an early age others go on being fairly ambidextrous until they are around 3 years old.

We so take our own skills for granted that we cut bread, lay tables, clean shoes, use scissors and comb our hair without really noticing which hand we use. Our children try to copy us, and since they are a bit clumsy in the early stages of learning any new skill it is often some time before it dawns on us that our child is trying to copy our right-handed usage of tools when his brain decrees that the other hand should be dominant; however children will find this out for themselves if they are allowed to experiment freely.

It is important that children are not pressured to change, for whether they are right- or left-handed is controlled by that part of the brain which controls language – talking, writing and reading – and any interference could lead to speech difficulties such as stammering, and later on to problems with reading and writing.

About 1 in 10 children is left-handed, a few more boys than girls, and heredity is a factor. My family is all right-handed, so are my husband and son, but our daughter is left-handed like her paternal grandmother. Left-handed children tend to take a little longer to learn new skills – no wonder, when everything is geared to a world of right-handed people. But now there are stockists who specialize in tools for left-handed people. (See *Useful Addresses*.)

STILLBIRTH AND NEONATAL DEATH

Few experiences are as shocking as a pregnancy that ends in the death of the baby. Heart, mind, body and soul have been preparing for life in the most personal way possible, and then there is not only no baby, but a dead baby. Sometimes the mother will be told that the baby within her has already died, which makes labour infinitely harder to endure. Sometimes the baby dies during or shortly after delivery. Sometimes the baby dies after delivery whilst still in hospital, either from causes unknown or from a terminal illness known from birth. Everyone around the mother has babies, and she has nothing.

Every year over 6,000 parents in the UK lose a baby because it is stillborn, and about the same number lose their babies after birth. The chances are that at some time in our lives it will happen to someone we know, and since the parents have to bear the full brunt of the suffering, the least we can do is to learn how to support them and how to avoid adding to their distress.

We need to understand that even if the baby is never seen, to the parents – and particularly to the mother – that baby was a real person. And the absence of that person has to be mourned as any other death in the family would be mourned.

In many ways it is even more upsetting because one's body can't switch-off motherhood, the milk is produced, and the longing to hold and cradle the baby is already there in arms that may literally ache. Most parents know instinctively that they want to hold their baby, even though lifeless or deformed. Mothers, some in their 60s and 70s, have commented on how much the holding comforted them, although those around them were shocked in those early days; and others have written to say they longed to, but weren't 'allowed'. Many who didn't want to at the time have regretted it later saying 'there was nothing to show that there had ever been a baby, even though to us he was a person,' or 'she was dead, but she was still part of us and we don't even know what she looked like.' Because of this some hospitals now take photographs of the baby, and have found that many parents who couldn't face seeing them at the time have been glad of them later.

There is no one 'right' or 'wrong' answer. Those involved with the birth and death must feel their way together towards the solution which allows individual parents – particularly the mother – to assuage their grief in their own way.

What is certain is that the time will come when the parents are home again, and have to face the world. And it is very hurtful to be ignored, or spoken to as though nothing has happened. It is also a strain on meeting people for the first time after the bereavement (any bereavement) having to wait, wondering when, if and how the matter will eventually be broached. It is best to say at once, 'I'm so sorry . . .' and to take it from there. Most mothers want to talk about it, some with tears, some with anger, and some with guilt, and all they ask of us is that we shall listen in supportive sympathy. It is better to say nothing than to offer such glib and pointless comments as, 'Still, you're young. You'll get over it . . . there will be other babies.' It was *this* baby they wanted. Neither is it wise to say, 'The best thing you can do is to have another to take your mind off it.' If a new baby is conceived too quickly the parents may not be in the state of physical and mental health that every new conception deserves. And experience suggests that if the new baby is born within a year or so of the loss of the last baby, then it may be more difficult to see the new arrival as a person unique in his or her own right rather than as a replacement for the one that was lost.

The mother may need to 'blame' someone, the doctor, the midwife, her mother or mother-in-law, her employer, her husband – just listen, but keep well clear of making judgements or taking sides. The chances are she is trying to explain it to herself, not to blame. Or she may be trying to avoid feelings of guilt in herself, 'What did I do, or not do, or eat, or drink, or lift, or inherit. . . .?' And here comfort and reassurance are in order.

But perhaps those most able to offer comfort are those who have been through the experience themselves and there are organizations – the Stillbirth and Neonatal Death Society and the Stillbirth and Perinatal Death Association – that can help with this, so do contact them. (See *Useful Addresses*.)

ESTABLISHING AN INTEREST IN COOKING AND GOOD FOOD

Recently I heard a Home Economics teacher talking to a group of mothers and fathers about cooking with young children. She endeared herself immediately by saying, 'We're not talking about teaching children to cook – we're talking about introducing children to the magic of cooking.'

Her own children are now 6 and 3, and she knew all about mess and muddle, and both wanting to 'help' together, and the enthusiasm that burns itself out before the clearing up. As she understood it all so well we opened up, and sat there mentally adapting it all to our own children and kitchens.

She cooked with her first child beside her, right from the highchair stage. It seemed natural to enjoy being together, and for a long while watching was enough to keep the onlooker happily absorbed.

'Experts' do rather go on these days about parents being their child's first and most important teachers, but this mother was wise enough to learn from her children rather than teach them. She watched her child's face, and began to see the cooking process through her child's eyes – not 'making a cake', but tipping a stream of shining white sugar out of a bag with a gentle wooshing sound: picking up an egg and banging it on the side of a bowl, to release something that didn't look in the least like the familiar boiled, poached, scrambled or fried egg: creaming the butter and sugar with a brown wooden spoon, hard going at first, and then easing into a rhythmic flop, flop; beating the eggs with a whisk, with a quicker, lighter flip, flip; sieving the flour in a soft silent cloud; cutting paper for the cake tin and snipping it round the edges before tucking it neatly into place. The child watched and listened so intently that her mother kept peacefully quiet at first, so that nothing should break into the fascination of those keenly focused senses. But later she tried a gentle running commentary, just enough to be natural and friendly without spoiling the continued pleasure of watching – 'now the sugar, and in it goes . . . there'.

Eventually the desire to watch led to the desire to join in, and by trial and error they discovered together what gave pleasure and satisfaction – greasing bun tins, and stirring the eggs with a fork so that the yolks broke and streaked into the slippery white. Slowly skills graduated to tipping sugar into the mixing bowl and adding the eggs her mother had finally whisked into a bubbling liquid.

The second child reached the watching stage, and the first went on to weighing and measuring. In answer to the query 'Do you teach her in pints and ounces, or litres and kilograms?' she delighted us by saying 'Neither at this stage, I just point to the mark and say "up to there".' At this stage the mother discovered it worked best to prepare the kitchen for cooking on her own – floor covered, table covered, all the utensils and ingredients to hand – before bringing in the children, rolling up their sleeves, washing their hands, putting on overalls, and settling one in the highchair and the other on a large solid tip-proof stool.

She also embarked upon mixed salads, not wanting the children only to love cooking sweet things. They shelled hard-boiled eggs, and mixed the yolk with grated cheese or salad cream before spooning it back; they shared the scrubbing, grating and arranging of carrots; the washing and pulling apart of lettuce leaves; the cutting of cold cooked potatoes with a blunt knife, turning them in salad cream and garnishing with cut parsley.

Throughout all these trials the mother kept to a few simple principals: the children need to be successful, therefore recipes needed to be simple and amenable to slow, hot, heavy handling: they needed to enjoy eating the result: and they needed to absorb incidentally an understanding of good basic nutrition.

A cloth was lifted from the table in front of us, to disclose a veritable feast cooked by her children for our benefit. Wholemeal rolls in the shape of snails, mice and hedgehogs; pinwheel sandwiches; cheese straws, twisted and glazed and sprinkled with poppy and sesame seeds; a fruit toss-in cake; lively hand-fashioned gingerbread men; and plates of mixed salad looking as pretty as a picture under their clingfilm cover.

Without being 'taught' these children have learned, with great enjoyment, to love cooking, and to know more about how to feed a family wisely and well than many an adult.

TREATS

A treat is an imaginative surprise that comes out of the blue – unexpected, unusual and for no particular reason.

I remember my first treat vividly. I was sitting in the big pram, with the hood half up, being taken for my afternoon walk. The pram stopped and there was a flurry of movement, talk and colour that I couldn't take in, but at the end of it mother handed me a windmill on a stick. I looked at it intently, and can see it now with the perfect clarity with which I saw it then: strips of bright blue celluloid, shaped, curved, folded and fastened to the stick with a long twist of thick wire. I lifted it up towards Mother, and the wind caught the sails. The blue shape disappeared in a whirling whirring clickety-click of paler blue haze at the top of the stick. I drew it closer to have another look, and in the shelter of the hood it was still again. Out and in, fast and still, clicking or silent – sheer magic. And *I* was the one who could make it happen at will.

Once my sister and I were looking through the window at the rain pouring down so hard it bounced up again. I said I wished I could take my clothes off and go out in it, and Mother said, 'Well, why not?' What a glorious treat! We can remember it now, stamping on the grass that was almost under water, and the feel of it on the soles of our feet; the force with which the rain hit us; the sensation of rain penetrating our hair to our scalps, and then our hair flowing down our faces. We were bombarded with sensations, and there came a wonderful moment when we were part of it all, dancing in the rain, free and exhilarated. Mother meanwhile had returned to the 'sensible' bit, so when it was all over she was there with towels and a hot bath to draw it all to a perfect conclusion.

A treat our own children loved was a ride on the Tuesday bus. We didn't 'go' anywhere. We just sat on the top front seats and watched the world go by. And half way round the circuit we had our packets of sandwiches and milk, and then got off at our starting point.

Often it was the children who gave us treats, and I remember a very special bunch of anemones, a sugar mouse, a pot of tea in bed made with (fairly) hot tap water, and a friend's torn raincoat brought back from school for me to mend (as a treat for the friend who was afraid to take it home).

Remember your own childhood treats. And if most children seem to have far more than you did remember, too, that only half the treat is what is actually given. *The other half is the change in our habitual response.*

If your usual greeting to a dirty child is 'Look at you! Wherever have you been?', give both of you a treat. Look at the happy face (instead of the dirty hands, knees and clothes) and smile back at it saying 'Hello! You look as though you've had a lovely time. What have you been doing?'

If you usually keep everybody hanging about waiting for you, give them a treat by being ready on time for once.

A treat is an expansive gesture of love towards another person. It means putting yourself in their place, and suddenly knowing what to do to give them that lovely 'lift' and response that is its own reward.

FINDING THE COURAGE TO STAND-UP FOR OUR CHILDREN

A recent meeting with a mother has lingered in my mind, for the answer to the question she asked lay so far back from the question itself.

There had been a school medical, and their daughter of 11 was found to need glasses. A prescription had been sent home in order that the glasses could be obtained, and the question was, 'Do you think I should get it made up?' The answer was so obviously Yes that it seemed likely there was more to this than met the eye. Perhaps she had no faith in the school doctor? But if that was so she could have taken her daughter to a local optician to have her eyes independently tested free of charge. Or did she think the doctor could be guilty of prescribing glasses which were unnecessary for his own benefit? But there wasn't any benefit; his salary didn't depend on the result of tests, and he didn't sell the glasses.

There had to be something behind it all, and eventually it came out almost as an afterthought, 'My husband says it's ridiculous, she doesn't need them.' She also volunteered the information that her husband had always worn glasses, not just for reading but all the time. So possibly he had inherited a weakness or abnormality of some kind, and somewhere at the back of his mind there may have lurked a feeling of guilt that it was his 'fault' if he had passed it on. Or perhaps he was upset at the thought of his daughter wearing glasses from the point of view of appearance. Or was he just being 'difficult'?

Still there was no mention of the child's point of view, the possibility that she couldn't see the blackboard properly, that she might have headaches about which she didn't want to complain, that she might not be seeing anything clearly and in focus. It was this which prompted the question, 'Sometimes a parent has to make a choice between her partner and her child. If it comes to this what will you do?'

And then it all came out. Her instinct was to get the glasses with all possible speed, but she didn't want to upset her husband. Reading between the lines her life-long habit was one of obedience, first to her parents, then to her husband. She dreaded scenes of any kind, and following in her mother's footsteps preferred to suffer silently rather than provoke anger, sarcasm or an atmospheric silence.

There will be some of you reading this who will be exasperated that any woman could be so inhibited that she couldn't stand up for herself – let alone her child. But the world is full of such women (and men) – and since I used to be one of them I know how desperately difficult it is to find the courage to become one's own person.

Overprotected, or dominated, children sometimes grow up to marry gentle caring partners, who share their fear that any emotional rocking of the boat might lead to aggression and the loss of love – but such couples would almost certainly have got the glasses for their child at once.

Others find themselves drawn to someone like their dominant parent, and actually choose to take the line of 'Anything you say, dear' – but this can damage both partners. One may become arrogant and a bully, the other may shrink in stature through loss of self-esteem; one may come to fear the other, who in turn despises the weakness which keeps that other subservient. Such parents could well be so involved in their own game that the glasses just become the opening of a new tactical war.

Fortunately for us all protective parental love is so strong that it can overcome all other instincts – even that of self-preservation. So it was for this mother. She suddenly said, 'I shall have to get them, shan't I?' And it wasn't a question, it was a statement. Then, she went on, 'We'll go after school – and I shan't say anything unless I'm asked. But whether he knows now or when the glasses come I shall just say it was a risk we couldn't take. And Tracy can tell us what sort of difference they make.'

She has taken the first step in finding the courage to put her child's needs before her own fear – the first step in rediscovering her own worth and self-esteem. And in offering the marriage a chance to grow up.

ESTABLISHING A BRIDGE BETWEEN HOME AND SCHOOL

The first memory many parents have is of their first day at school, and now for some of you this day is arriving for your child. Starting school is just as much a landmark for parents as it is for children, and some of you may be surprised at the intensity of your own feelings as the day approaches.

You may be fearful that your child isn't quite ready to cope without you for a whole day. You may dread his or her distress at the moment of parting, yet know that you could be hurt if your inseparable companion dived into this new experience without a backward glance. You may feel a sense of loss as your 'baby' prepares to leave you. Or you may be longing for the day when at last you will have a few hours to be yourself, to think your own thoughts, and to be free of the constant responsibility for another human life. Whatever your feelings are accept them, but keep them to yourself or share them with those who have been through it all before you.

Your child may also have feelings that surface unexpectedly. One child was found deep in thought sitting on the loo, and her mother was greeted with, 'I've just thought . . . whatever will you do without me all day?' Her mother said, 'I shall miss you very much, but I shall . . .' and she went through all the familiar daily doings ending with 'And then I shall come to school to meet you and bring you home for tea.'

Another child who had been looking forward to the great day suddenly began to cry at bedtime. He clung like a limpet and sobbed 'Won't I be able to come home even *once* before I'm eleven?' When the mystery was unravelled his mother remembered saying to a neighbour in his hearing 'We're lucky. The school where David is going will keep him until he's eleven.'

Keep calm on the day, neither over-jolly nor anxious, least of all tearful; if tears are to be shed do it over a cup of coffee when you get home. And be happily undemanding when you meet each other again.

You have probably imagined a happy child rushing to tell you all the news of the day, whereas you will probably be met by a small, silent, thirsty, overtired, dishevelled little object with a distinct tendency to be grumpy. If so, then go home together in comfortable quietness and offer a drink of water before anything else. Often children don't like to ask for more water at dinner, and don't yet know how to get it at any other time. Possible dehydration needs to be dealt with before teatime can be enjoyed as a winding-down time for both of you.

If your eager question 'What have you been doing today?' is met with 'Nothing', try not to feel let-down or shut-out. For days, or even weeks, young children often experience 'home' and 'school' as two different worlds, and it takes time for each to be carried over into the other.

Now for practicalities. Children's greatest anxiety centres round the lavatory. Where is it? Who will show me? Do I have to wait? Who and how do I ask? Will they understand our family's language for this function? You must both be sure of the answers to *all* these questions on your first visit to the school.

Children also need the confidence of knowing that they can dress, undress, change and fasten shoes without help if necessary.

And don't be late collecting them – one child expressed the fear of many when he said, 'Do you think she's forgotten I'm here?'

For children already at school the new term may bring a change of teacher, class or even school. And we are apt to overlook the anxiety that these changes may cause some children; would any of us be completely unmoved by a change of boss, neighbours or job?

There isn't one of us who doesn't remember from our own experience how heavily dependent our success in any subject was upon whether or not we liked the teacher, and whether or not we felt he or she liked us. In the first few years at school this is particularly true, and we should *listen* to what our children tell us about their teachers. We are not required to take sides, or to offer platitudes about it being six of one and half a dozen of the other, or moral lectures about not telling tales. They just want us to listen sympathetically while they pour it all out. And if we understand what they are saying we may be able to lighten the load on bad days by saying first, 'What's Old Beastly been up to today?', so that the recital can get off to a cheerfully indignant start.

But if anxiety and distress begins to mount, together with a reluctance to go to school, then something should be done. Where are children to turn if not to their parents? The difficulty lies in doing it in such a way that it neither rebounds on the child, nor labels us as fussy parents or trouble makers.

Depending on the size of the school, the nature of the difficulty, and the amount of courage available, do talk things over with the headteacher, or the class teacher. As a teacher myself I know how valuable it was when a parent said, 'Can you spare a moment? There seems to be a crossed line somewhere . . .' or 'Ann is really very worried, could we try to get to the bottom of it together?' or 'I know it may sound daft but William is frightened of you' or 'Couldn't you praise her sometimes? She's losing heart.'

Being human, it helped if in their first sentence parents made it clear that they were with, rather than against, me. I could then listen to what they were saying – and respond. Both as a teacher and parent I have found this works well. None of us is infallible, we all need to be 'told' from time to time.

School is for learning about relationships as well as subjects, and teachers and parents need to work in partnership.

THOUGHTS ON WORK

We urgently need to re-examine certain familiar words to which false and outdated images are still attached – words like work, job, professional, vocation, employment and unemployment.

In the old days it was generally assumed that 'going to work' meant manual work, and that it was done by those on the lower rungs of the social ladder. If you were a rung or two higher you 'had a job', and probably went to an office or a shop in clean and tidy clothes. If you were 'a professional person' you were known to have had years of training, had passed exams, and were deemed to be not only cleverer but somehow *better* than those below you on this pernicious ladder, which stood like an invisible status symbol in the midst of each community.

Those who 'had a vocation' felt called upon to be of service to mankind, and they were credited with the ability to move up and down the ladder and perch alongside anyone on any rung – these included doctors, nurses, and men of the Church. On the other hand, some had a vocation to music, painting or other innate talent which they felt it their responsibility to fulfil – and they were allowed to dissociate themselves from contact with anyone on any rung of this wretched ladder. They were pictured as sitting on little clouds floating at some distance from real people – though anyone was free to look, listen and be inspired (if they had eyes to 'see' and ears to 'hear').

But what about mothers and children – where did they fit in on this ladder? Children often show us their understanding of the situation in their play. In any nursery or playgroup you can see them in the home corner, cooking and eating imaginary meals, bustling about, loving, nagging and slapping their doll-children, talking to each other – and then the Daddy (who may be a boy or a girl) says, 'Well, I'm off to work . . .' and gathering up his lunchbox or briefcase, off he goes. He erupts out of the front door with great purpose and style . . . and then it all fizzles out. What is work? What do you do? Where do you go? They know it is important, and that you go out to do it. But what, exactly, is 'work'?

A judge once showed where he, too, fizzled out in understanding, when he said of the mother of ten standing before him in court, 'She hasn't a job, I gather?' to which the creditable reply was, 'Your Honour, she has ten children . . .'

It is time we all reviewed our own daily round, whatever and wherever it may be – factory, home, office, school – and asked ourselves questions about 'work', 'jobs' and 'being at home'.

A job is a task that has to be done. Work is the application of effort to a purpose. We *all* work, we *all* have jobs to do (whether or not they are paid), and those jobs are what we make them. Not only that, the way in which we do them makes *us*.

Something has gone terribly wrong when those who are unemployed feel that they have lost their self-respect when they lost their jobs, for the two are not indivisible – unless years of conditioning going right back to childhood have made them so.

Unemployment is a tragedy and a waste; loss of income is desperate for some, and worrying for all. I see men and women cut off in their prime, the children of my friends eager to leave school or college and 'start living' – and my heart goes out to them all. But a deeper honesty raises other questions which relate to our real worth in the community, and the real root of our self-respect.

A booklet came my way the other day talking about the cost of having children, and among other things it referred to the cost to the country of having women tied up at home doing dirty and boring jobs like washing nappies – which could be done by someone else, while the mother did more useful things elsewhere.

But this is the old thinking, not new. It is back to that wretched ladder – but this time it rears its menacing shadow inside the home instead of outside it – with the lower rungs relegated to lesser mortals who are only fit for dirty, boring manual jobs like nappy changing, while the superior beings go out to climb the other ladder. It just won't do.

Hundreds of thousands of mothers, and a growing number of fathers, have a real vocation for parenthood – a strong natural calling from within, not just a response to social pressure, or conformity to their upbringing, or submission to the economic convenience of the State, or any of that claptrap. These parents *want* to make a physical and emotional commitment to one partner, they *want* to have children – and they know perfectly well that the job of parenthood entails dirty manual work, endless repetitive jobs, overwork, and curtailment of their personal freedom for quite some time. These are the ones who don't mind changing nappies because if you love someone you don't want them to be wet or dirty and uncomfortable. They take the mess and the smell in their stride, and use the job as an opportunity for a kiss and a cuddle, a chat and a kick on the floor – knowing perfectly well that they aren't just nappy changing but are laying the foundation of their baby's life in a relationship of love, play and caring. All of which adds up to work.

But having said that, it must also be said that babies need to be brought up to want to help others in exactly the same spirit of caring. It is quicker and easier to do jobs without their well-meaning efforts to help us, and to 'work' without interruption, but if we don't help them to gain value in their own eyes, and in ours, during the common round of daily tasks, isn't this the beginning of their need to find 'jobs' and 'work' outside the home to confirm their worth?

For children, play *is* their work, and they could teach us a thing or two. We tend to divide our lives into work and recreation, whereas they can show us (if we haven't deflected the course of true play too badly) that life can be lived in a continuous rhythm of work and re-creation – according to what is being done, and the spirit in which it is being done at the time.

The problems of unemployment have to be thought about together with the use of leisure, and the roots of our sense of worth.

PART TWO

ESTABLISHING GUIDELINES FOR FAMILY LIFE

BEDTIME

Somehow parents feel they are expected to end each day by leading compliant children upstairs for a leisurely bath, followed by a peaceful bedtime story, a goodnight kiss, and sweet dreams until the morning.

But reality isn't often like that. Everyone is tired, toys, pieces of Leggo are everywhere, the kitchen in chaos, and there is yet another meal to prepare. As the pace quickens tempers fray, and bedtime can become a battle of wits and wills.

The major cause of conflict is often timing. How would you feel if someone suddenly announced, 'Come on, we're going out!' just when you were lost in a book, or in the middle of a job that was going well? The chances are you would feel resentful, and protest. So it is with children. Although it may not look as though they are doing anything much, they can be lost in their own world. And if we jolt them back into ours too suddenly, they protest.

Always give them at least ten minutes warning before bedtime. This gives them time to finish what they are doing. But if they are deeply immersed in their play, or if there is a great deal to put away, then even ten minutes may not be enough. Give an earlier warning, and be prepared to help *slowly* with the putting away if the task is too daunting.

In early childhood clearing up is an important part of the winding down process of play. The trouble is we are in such a perpetual hurry ourselves that it is easier to clear up after them than to slow down to help them.

Children have no sense of clock time, and we confuse them still further by saying 'I'll come in a minute', when we mean no such thing. It will take time for them – and perhaps even for you – to learn how long ten real minutes are.

If we can learn to plan ahead to give children more time for almost everything we want them to do we can accomplish just as much, with far less wear and tear on our nervous systems. This is particularly true at bedtime, but it can also benefit our whole way of living.

BATHTIME

On a bad day bathtime feels like the last hurdle in the Grand National – one final effort before the winning post of bed. Chaos reigns in the kitchen, a trail of toys lies everywhere, there has been a battle of wits and wills to get the children to the bathroom – and they fiddle about instead of getting undressed. If we dash to fetch clean nightclothes then on our return the bath towels lie in a soggy heap, drenched by a tidal wave, and one child is crying because her hair is wet as well.

On these days there is a hasty rub-over with a soapy flannel, a quick rinse, and OUT – protestations or not. And with grim determination we try to contain in a clean dry towel what feels like a yelling squirming octopus, trying to dry the various arms and legs before stuffing them into nightclothes and bed.

On a good day we can chat or sing our way upstairs, and give them all the time they need to do all the things we remember doing at their age. Time to float and sink the duck with a hole in it, and fail to sink the new one which pops straight up to the surface however many times we push it down to the bottom. Time to float on our elbows, and 'swim' under the bath rack. Time to scrub the side of the bath with the nailbrush, and to lose the soap in the water become cloudy with soapsuds. So much time that the water grew chilly, and we plastered wet flannels on our chests, only to learn that the momentary warmth was followed by a more penetrating cold. Then the plug was pulled, and there was the last minute scramble to be lifted out before we went down the plughole.

We need to remember our childhood for it is these shared memories which bring us close to our children. If we can share memories of what we did, then we can also share with them how we felt, this helps them to identify with us as people.

Mother used to say, 'If you start and end the day clean, I don't mind what happens in the middle,' and I suppose most of us see bathtime as a practical way of removing the day's grime before getting into a clean bed – with playtime in the bath as a bonus.

But for children bathtime can be more than this. It is very important for children's mental health that they are allowed to get dirty during their play, and just as important to discover that dirt washes off. There is great satisfaction in the magic of 'now it's dirty, now it's clean', and children need to confirm this understanding by washing and scrubbing all sorts of objects and surfaces as well as themselves. This is particularly important for children who are brought up to equate dirtiness with naughtiness: they must be able to feel 'good' again. So their washing of themselves and other objects is a way of saying, 'I can make dirtiness and naughtiness, but I can also make cleanliness and goodness.'

The bad days are the very ones that need to end on a warm, peaceful, optimistic note. If the day has been full of upsets leading to bad feelings about everybody and everything, then a warm relaxing bath can wash it all away.

Never withhold the goodnight kiss, which says, 'It's been a bad day, but I love you, and we'll start again tomorrow.'

WAITING FOR BLADDER AND BOWEL CONTROL

A well-known television personality mentioned on one programme that all her children had been potted before they were fifteen minutes old. This seemed such an insensitive reaction to the miracle of birth that I couldn't help wondering whether, fifteen seconds after conception, she had said, 'Did you put the cat out?'

Parents tend to worry unduly about the age when their children 'should' be dry, and 'ought' to use the pot. Very few 2-year-olds are dependable by day, and certainly not at night; 10 per cent of 5-year-olds are still not dry at night, and 5 per cent of 10-year-olds.

Think of it from the child's point of view. Babies have no control over anything but their sucking and clinging reflexes when they are born. It takes months to discover, and use, their hands purposefully; and one or two years to develop the strength, balance and control to use their feet and legs for walking confidentally. How much more difficult it must be to control muscles that you can't see, and don't even know you've got.

The waste products of food are excreted in urine and faeces, which accumulate in the bladder and bowel until these become so full that they are emptied by a natural reflex action. But it can take some children more than a couple of years to recognize the sensations which will eventually lead to an unaccompanied trip to the potty or loo (and even then they will sometimes find that they have left it too late).

We need to be patient and flexible, and refuse to enter into competition with other parents on this score. Children have different sized bladders, different appetites, different thirsts, from each other, and these factors also differ from day to day in each child. On a hot day water is lost in perspiration, and if we don't offer water freely there will be less urine to pass. Or diet may lack enough roughage on some days, so the muscles of the bowel wall haven't enough to work on, then the residue stays in the bowel, where it becomes progressively harder until eventually it is passed with considerable pain. A toddler may understandably think, 'It hurts when I sit on the pot and do what I'm supposed to do, so I shan't sit on it again.' Not naughty but intelligent, and a signal to us that baked beans on wholemeal toast may give the bowels a chance to function more easily (but excessive amounts of beans can lead to the pain of wind, so continue to watch and learn).

Babies have enough to contend with in the first two years of life without us hurrying them to achieve adult standards of behaviour.

There is no magic right way, but there are certain hints and tips which may be helpful as you work things out for yourselves. It does no harm to have a potty around so that it is a familiar part of the bathroom scene. And if you feel you must start to use it early, then for goodness' sake don't think of it as 'training', only as familiarization. But be human about this – would you want to emerge from a warm bath, and a satisfying warm feed, to find that not only had someone let the draught in but was clamping a cold potty on to you? A few seconds contact with a warm potty won't do any harm (or much good either), as long as you don't continue with it if there is resistance. If you are 'lucky', all well and good, but don't imagine it is more than luck, which may or may not be repeated successfully during the following months.

If you are content to change nappies for as long as it takes your child to begin to recognize the signs of his own inner activity, then somewhere between one and two years you may be able to offer a pot in time for connections to be made. The running water of a bath sometimes triggers the bladder to work, and if a pot is at hand as the taps begin to flow you may be 'lucky', but a sudden move in this direction can also stop the flow of urine in mid-stream, which can be so painfully distressing that a re-release isn't achieved until the child is immersed in the warm water of the bath (a child's peace of mind and body is more important than hygiene at such times).

Similarly, if a child turns red and grunts then it may be a sign that the bowel muscles are beginning to constrict, and a pot may be just the thing for his or her comfortable evacuation.

Summer time is the easiest for learning to go without nappies, for with nothing more than knickers to cope with it is easier for bottoms and pots to make successful contact and nothing succeeds like success.

A 2-year-old of my acquaintance refused to use his pot until he spent the day with two children of about his own age. He watched them perform with interest, and next day said, 'Lindy . . . potty . . .' and literally ran to get his own – and performed triumphantly. Everything came together in his mind, he suddenly 'knew' what it was all about.

On the other hand, a mother told of her child who was allowed to empty both bladder and bowel in their large garden during the summer – and was pleased when he chose a certain bush to disappear behind at regular intervals. But she was less enthusiastic when winter came, for he refused to go anywhere else – rain, frost or snow, he demanded to go out to his bush. And when the tension mounted he was also discovered trying to get out during the night. He had 'trained' himself all too well, by creating a habit which became more deeply reinforced each time it was repeated.

It seems wisest to strike a happy medium, by offering a potty from time to time, but to be relaxed about the whole question of wet or dirty nappies. And although it would be helpful to have a dry, clean first child before the second one is born, it really is unwise to exert any pressure at such a sensitive time in family life.

LEARNING TO GET DRESSED

A Japanese playgroup mother came to a social evening in her beautiful national costume, and admiration and interest was so great that she promised to bring it into the playgroup the next morning for the children to see, and the mothers to try on. It looked so easy as she slipped into it and deftly wrapped and tucked the wide sash around her. But no one could follow her example. It was amazing how slow and clumsy normally deft fingers became, and how chastened and inadequate people suddenly felt.

Yet their difficulty was as nothing compared to that of children learning to dress themselves. Children's hands and wrists aren't yet strong, their fingers and thumbs aren't very good at working independently, or doing precisely what they want them to do. And they are no more certain about which garment goes where, and how, than most of us are certain of the way when we first learn to drive; 'But you've been there dozens of times, you *must* know the way' we hear, to which we feebly reply, 'I know, but I was always watching the view, not the route.'

Next time your child spills something down him which necessitates a change of t-shirt or jumper try an observation check. Help to remove the wet or dirty garment, and – making sure that the atmosphere between you is warm, friendly and relaxed – offer the clean one with a casual, 'Pop it on while I just . . .' Then watch carefully out of the corner of your eye as you pretend to get on with something else.

Some children may dive into a clean t-shirt comparatively easily. Some will spread it on the floor and contemplate the various holes for head, arms and body as though making a mental map of the lay-out. Some will pick it up, plonk it on their heads, and tug, which results in a baffling bonnet-effect. Some will find two holes through which two arms are thrust, without realizing that one is through the armhole and the other through the neck.

Some will pull the garment over their heads, and then be unable to find any opening for their arms as they pull at the unwieldy folds of material under their chins, and if they eventually find one armhole it is almost impossible to make the garment stretch enough to push the second arm and elbow through.

Buttons are particularly difficult. When you dress them a compliant body stands there, looking down in a turned-off sort of way, while your fingers do a lightening twist or two and, hey presto, they're done up. But left alone to the task things are very different. One hand for the bit with the hole in it, the other to hold the button and steer it with great concentration into the hole . . . good . . . then leave it there in order to move your hand to the other side of the hole and pull the button through . . . The idea is good, but that isn't the way buttons behave left to their own devices.

Do watch your children *very* carefully sometimes. Appreciate their difficulties, respect their efforts, marvel at their patient perseverance, and offer help before they give up in defeat or frustration.

The foundation of their attitude to life and learning is being laid, day by day, according to your attitude to their clumsiness, slowness and success in learning new skills. They are not just learning to dress, they are learning to learn. And their incentive to learning is the twin pleasure of their parents' approval of their efforts and the heightening of their self-esteem as they master new skills.

COPING WITH FINICKY EATERS

Children vary in their eating habits as widely as in everything else. Some children eat anything and everything; some make no fuss but are incredibly slow; some have fads and fancies; some 'won't eat anything'; some are messy to the point of the revulsion of the onlooker. If your child is a poor eater in one way or another it isn't the slightest bit of use anyone saying 'Don't worry', because nothing worries parents as much as children who won't eat.

There is a very deep instinct linking the giving of food with the giving of love, and if children refuse the food that has been painstakingly prepared and offered to them it is upsetting at two levels. Parents feel hurt and angry because it seems as though both they and their food are being rejected; and they can also be frightened in case their child comes to harm. Guilt adds to the mounting tension for it seems to parents that they are failures in this aspect of mothering or fathering. As one mother put it, 'I dread mealtimes and begin to get wound up even before I dish up.'

If you are currently anxious, baffled or angry take heart, so are thousands of other parents, and it is extremely unlikely that your child will come to any harm.

Sometimes children develop a craving for certain foods, like the one I knew who refused everything but tomato ketchup on dry bread for weeks and apparently came to no harm. Quite often a child will know instinctively what to eat, but just check with your doctor if the craving is persistent or unusual, for example an excessive amount of salt.

But sometimes it is a way of saying, 'You are hurrying me too hard and fast. I can't cope with all these "musts" and "oughts" relating to so many different looks, feels and tastes of new foods. I shall stick to what I like and feel safe with.' If so, take the pressure off. Accept the situation, but make it easy for the child to opt in again without losing face. After a day or two you could try saying, kindly but casually, 'I'll put a sausage (or cube of cheese, piece of banana or something that used to be enjoyed) on this little saucer near you in case you feel extra hungry.' If it is untouched don't comment, just eat it casually as you clear the table and try again a few meals later, still without comment, and avoiding at all costs making an 'atmosphere'.

Sometimes a child 'won't eat' for one reason or another, and we may find ourselves reduced to endless games, 'One spoonful for Grandad . . . now one for Auntie . . . and one for Fido . . . and one last tiny one for that little bird outside.' Or we dig trenches through the potato to let the gravy through, until one day something snaps and we say, 'Right! You're not getting down until you *do* eat it.' And at that point food becomes the issue for a clash of wills, instead of the symbol of friendship which has always been associated with the breaking of bread together throughout history.

If you have reached this point, then forgive and forget, and start again. Be reassured that children won't come to any harm if they go without food for a day or two, as long as they have plenty of water to drink. So calm yourself, prepare very easy meals, and invite your child to share them. If he or she doesn't want any just say, 'All right, if you're not hungry would you like to get down and play?' Eat your meal peacefully, and clear it away, with nothing on offer until the next meal. Whether your child is temporarily off food, or (subconsciously) having you on, it is almost certain that if you don't allow yourself to become emotionally involved the child will begin to eat again. When this happens refrain from drawing attention to it – just be glad for both of you.

One last reminder, milk is a *food*. Sometimes parents express anxiety about the fact that their child doesn't eat anything, and then say, 'Still, at least there's no lack of enthusiasm for milk, so that's something.' If a child is getting all the nourishment needed in this form there will be little or no incentive to satisfy natural hunger with other foods.

The relaxed offering of ordinary food and drink at mealtimes, with no tension or anxiety to create a block in the child's mind as each meal approaches, solves most problems. But if you feel sure you are all relaxed, and your child still doesn't show any interest in food, and has no energy, then go to the doctor.

THOUGHTS ON SWEET-EATING

Addiction to sugar is just as real, and just as difficult to break, as addiction to alcohol or smoking. What they all have in common is a short-term pleasure accompanied by long-term damage, so moderation is the watchword – together with an understanding of our own sweet-eating pattern.

Many people can take them or leave them. Some people never have sweets in the house, either because they are adamant that they are not going to start the habit in their children, or because they are not interested enough to buy them. Others buy a supply once a week, and when they've gone they've gone. Some buy on impulse occasionally, eat the lot and then don't want any more for weeks. Some crave them all the time, and if this is part of a weight problem the support of a slimming group may be needed.

But probably the most usual pattern is for people not to bother about them until they get a sudden craving triggered by tiredness or stress. On the last leg of a hike, or a late journey home after working late, or a day's decorating, sweets can release a quick supply of energy until a meal and relaxation are available. Stress is more complicated for our bodies often have no need, although 'we' most certainly have! We may feel we are under attack, like a besieged building in danger of collapse; or we may have given all we've got quite freely. But the result is the same – the need to fill-up, either to withstand the pressure or to replenish supplies.

Listening to parents over the years it seems that 'thick' sweets fill this need better than clear ones. Barley sugar may be recommended for quick energy, but it is usually a Mars bar that is wanted, or a hunk of chocolate cake, because it fills and satisfies by 'feel' as well as taste and calorific content.

It is difficult to distinguish the psychological craving for sweet things and the body's need to get the energy it needs quickly. What is certain is that we often lead children into some of our own traps unwittingly.

Because of our own associations between sweets, pleasure and comfort, it is all too easy to start the habit of giving our children sweets for treats, sweets for rewards, and sweets for comfort. And children in their turn come to associate sweets with pleasure and comfort. In fact, our praise and pleasure, reassurance, comforting cuddles or a distraction (not out of a paper bag or wrapper) meets their emotional needs much better – it is *us* they need, not our sweets.

It's worth remembering this because once we start the habit it leads to others that are no pleasure to anyone. On bad days, when we dash to the biscuit tin for ourselves, our children are likely to be whining and difficult, so then we give them sweets to pacify them for *our* sake. Sweets become bribes, and we all know where that leads!

Once the habit of sweet-eating is firmly established, requests may quickly turn to demands, and sweets can become the battleground for a power struggle. If this happens it needs to be resolved, long term, over a wider field. But meanwhile, under pressure, you may both crave something sweet. Have a picnic with thick sandwiches of fresh wholemeal bread and butter or margarine lightly spread with golden syrup. Very satisfying in bulk, feel and sweetness!

If you have a baby, do try not to encourage a sweet tooth, for it is likely to become painful for you both in different ways.

The safeguarding of children's teeth is important, but it is only one of many reasons for the need to think carefully about the time, place and amount of sweets in a happy, healthy, balanced childhood.

THE RESPONSIBLE USE OF TELEVISION

In most families now television is here to stay. We already know that some programmes are unsuitable viewing for children, and that any easy pleasure can become addictive – the old adage 'use it or lose it' applies to the use of our minds as well as our muscles or skills – so let us consider some of the good uses to which it can be put.

Sharing a programme can heighten communication between parents and children – under certain conditions. Children value the 'I'm with you' feeling that comes with sitting together in peaceful harmony, enjoying each other, the programme, and each other's enjoyment of the programme (to read the paper while the children watch conveys our disinterest and detachment from them as well as the programme).

Young children may watch intently for a short while and say 'Postman Pat!' in joyful recognition, and enjoy it if we say 'Yes', rather than distract them by adding 'He is working hard, isn't he?' or 'What's he doing now?' They want us to be *with* them, not leading them. For this reason I feel it is unfair to bombard them with questions at the end of a programme, though if it is turned off at the end, and we sit down with them again and re-establish the intimacy by saying something like 'He did have to drive a long way, didn't he?' the child will sometimes talk about what has just been seen. And we should *listen*, because the links being made may be very personal, and it may be these thoughts and feelings which need to be talked about, not the programme at all.

Children vary greatly in their ability to cope with tension and every child has periods when he or she is more vulnerable than usual, or particularly susceptible to something for personal reasons. So we have to learn when to break the tension, and when to use the off-switch. In general, children need to learn that life is full of ups and downs, fears and joys, goodies and baddies, and that tension is followed by relief far more often than by disaster.

If they are enjoying a programme, but their faces indicate that the tension is becoming unmanageable, we can lessen it without interrupting the flow of the story just by moving, or if necessary by bringing them right back to reality by saying something like, 'I expect they are already on their way to find her, don't you?'

As children grow older we need to explain about actors and acting, so that they understand how accidents, fires, floods, illness and death are stage-managed. And that blood isn't blood, and swords don't really go into people. Then, if they have reached the stage of being concerned about the people who are killed, we can say at the appropriate moment, 'Now *he* can get up, and have a wash, and put on his own clothes, and go home!' Children need help to bridge the gap between reality and illusion, but only you will know how and when to do it without spoiling their over-all enjoyment.

For some children there is a sense of compulsion to go on watching something that frightens them, and I think this is when they need us to set a personal example by saying, 'I'm not enjoying this, let's turn it off and do something else.' And do just that. Your child may not be able to let go immediately, and there will possibly be remonstrations about 'I want it' or even 'You always spoil everything, you never let me have anything I want to have.' Don't take this personally for it probably means they are still anxious about what was going to happen next (this can be worked out between you), or else they are trying to hide their relief by a show of bravado.

If we set the example on our own behalf – rather than switch-off arbitrarily on their behalf – we are helping them to become selective according to their own needs and feelings.

Television can be a bridge between our children and ourselves in all sorts of ways, but ultimately we have the responsibility of deciding how much our children view, and when, and what is to be banned and why.

FAIRNESS AND EQUALITY

Children have a strong sense of what is fair and what isn't, but the cry, 'It isn't fair' doesn't always mean what we think. Quite often what they are saying is, 'You haven't behaved with equality', and that boils down to 'You have favoured one of us above the other, and that must mean you love one more than the other. I haven't got a fair share of your love.'

Children have a wonderful sense of fair play, but even when they accept that something is 'fair', and will therefore hold no grudges, that doesn't always stop them from making a bit of a scene at the time; emotions are so much stronger than intellect.

Two incidents at the Child Guidance Clinic many years ago have stayed with me. An undersized and fragile 9-year-old came with his loving but harassed little mother each week, because he still couldn't read a word. It wasn't that he didn't have the intelligence, but that the intelligence he had was blocked because he was permanently anxious and bewildered. After a term he had lost his fear of failing in our particular room, and by the second term he could read very simple books with pride and pleasure. He also enjoyed playing with the Scrabble board and some of the letters (though we didn't attempt to play Scrabble). About this time his mother said she had a problem which she wanted to discuss privately as it concerned Christmas presents. Her elder son wanted a bike, and Chris wanted Scrabble, but in those days the bike cost £14 and the Scrabble £1, and she couldn't afford to give Chris something else for the £13 it would cost 'to be fair'.

At the same time another mother was troubled by the same dilemma, one child wanted a bike, the other wanted a guinea pig.

We all got together to discuss it. Both parents said they had always been fair over money, and always spent exactly the same on each child. But that wasn't the kind of equality each child wanted *on this occasion*. Each wanted his heart's desire, but both mothers agreed that if the children discovered later that one present had cost more than the other, then they would feel guilty. Yet they also agreed that they wouldn't feel guilty if they discussed it with their children beforehand, and if the children said that they wanted what they truly wanted – regardless of money. Both parents then had a different anxiety, what would grandparents, friends and relations say when they saw this apparent inequality of presents!

Fear of being thought unfair was something they dreaded, but they suddenly saw that they could simply explain how the decision had been reached – because it was fair according to the children.

Helping children to understand the fairness of meeting needs is important. Babies need more of our time, but this can be balanced by meeting the attention needs of the older child with times of special togetherness (the quality of these times is more important than their length). Whatever their age children need identical spending money at the fair, because roundabouts and dodgem cars cost the same whatever their age. If both children love ices, then each must have one, but if one hates ices then a packet of crisps would be 'fair'. Fairness and equality aren't always quite the same thing.

Sometimes there is a decision not to be *simultaneously* fair or equal which lies with neither parent nor child, but with a third party. Grandparents can surely be allowed to claim the privilege of age to say, as my mother used to, 'I love them and want them to stay, but I can't have both together. It's too much for me. The responsibility, and the mental effort to devote myself to them both, and their perfectly natural squabbles and energy, wear me out. So let them come one at a time.' This worked beautifully. The children understood, and each looked forward to being 'special' in turn. And since the one left at home was able to feel 'special' too (because one is usually easier than two or more!) there was never any comparing of notes afterwards on the score of fairness.

The *intention* to be fair must be seen and felt at all times. My sister and I remember our parents as being paragons of fairness, but we both vividly remember the day our father said, 'Your mother and I will always try to be fair, but don't expect *life* to be fair, because it isn't.'

This is a very hard lesson to learn, but being a farmer's daughter helped. When thousands of lettuce seedlings have been back-breakingly transplanted by hand from the seed bed to the open field, it isn't 'fair' when a sharp late frost kills them overnight. It isn't 'fair' when one child is more beautiful or gifted than another in the same family and it is even more 'unfair' if adults make these kind of comparisons. But what remains true is that with our help, our children can grow up to be happy with themselves and their lives – in spite of all inequalities.

COPING WITH DISTURBED EVENINGS

If children are good sleepers then few moments are more exquisite than those experienced when you are able to take time for yourself, having tucked them up for the night. The hurly-burly of the day is over. You can feel the 'self' within begin to expand as you let go mentally, and know that any jobs still lying in wait for you can be done with your hands and eyes only – easy, often positively therapeutic as you bridge the gap between the children's day and your own personal evening.

This doesn't mean that we don't love our children, and want to be rid of them. It just means that we've given them all we've got, and now we need to unwind and replenish our own depleted reserves before we, too, go to bed.

But no two children are alike, and even those who most resemble dormice can go through phases of having disturbed evenings. We all know the pattern. Just as we begin to relax there is the thunder of tiny feet overhead. We go to the foot of the stairs and call out (very nicely), 'What are you doing? Get back into bed and go to sleep.' Silence. Then the scampering begins again. We call out a second time, rather more firmly. This may do the trick, or a third disturbance may send us upstairs – on a good night to tuck them in firmly but soothingly with explanations about poor tired fathers needing peace and quiet (never a word about us), but on a bad night to tuck them in tight as Egyptian mummies with dire threats (we're only human).

Somehow it becomes a battle of wills and a trial of strength, which exhausts us still further without achieving its aims – no one can 'make' anybody go to sleep.

If we have had periods of insomnia ourselves we know how elusive sleep can be and how useless it is to be told, 'For goodness' sake stop tossing and turning and go to sleep' – we've been telling ourselves that for hours. Often the best thing to do is not to try, but to give up and read until sleep overtakes us.

So it is with children. Try saying, 'If you're not ready to go to sleep yet, look at your books. Here, let me pile up the pillow and make a nice nest so that it's all warm and cosy.' Go to the library together to choose 'bedtime books' quite openly, and as frequently as necessary. And choose a bedside lamp together (the angle-poise variety give good light to prevent eye strain), partly to heighten the impressions of a small secret world of their own in the darkened room, and partly to give the necessary self-control of knowing when to switch off literally and metaphorically. If your child isn't interested in books, then try jigsaw puzzles on a tray.

Another pattern is for the silence of the evening to be broken by the flinging open of the door through which the child erupts like Sammy Davis Junior, compelling attention by the force of personality and magnetic energy. This is the attention seeker, and nothing is more demoralizing than for the act to fall flat. The best way to combat this is for those of you downstairs to work out a counter-act of your own, and plan to put it into action on an evening when there is nothing you specially want to see on the television. When the star of the show bursts in take absolutely no notice, wait a few seconds, then one of you turn off the television, and both disappear behind books or the paper, or have a casually determined conversation about house insurance, or the local refuse collection. Just treat the intruder as you would a fly, keep it off you without swotting it. The chances are that eventually the child will fall asleep in a chair or on the floor, or creep back to bed. Acts need audiences.

But be alert to the child who truly does need attention, especially if you are aware of the fact that you aren't (because you can't for one of very many reasons) giving him or her the time, attention, love or understanding that is needed. Either make more time, or seek help from the Child Guidance Clinic, before there are other problems springing from the child's feeling of deprivation.

REALISTIC EXPECTATIONS OF TABLE MANNERS

I have yet to meet the parents who didn't care about their children's table manners. Partly this is our own childhood training reasserting itself automatically, but also there is the parental pride factor: if our children behave badly at meal-times, either in public or private company, we feel it implies that they have been 'badly brought up'. And we don't want to be judged and found wanting.

But look at it from the child's point of view, bearing in mind that example is the most powerful form of teaching, and that we offer ourselves as an example several times a day. We say, 'You can't get down until you've finished,' but how many meals do we sit through without jumping up and down, half a dozen times? We say, 'Elbows in!' But how can you avoid your elbows sticking out like wings when the table is chest high? We say, 'Sit up straight,' but which of us does? We say, 'Eat it slowly,' but how often have we fed them too quickly in the past? We popped one spoonful in, and then loaded the next one in anticipation, quite often lifting it to their mouths, or even touching their lips if they were slowing down, saying 'Come on.' Didn't we . . . anyway sometimes?

We say, 'Shut your mouth when you're eating,' but you can't if your nose is blocked, and it takes time to learn how to blow your nose satisfactorily.

We say, 'Don't stretch,' but if our own manners were up to scratch they wouldn't need to, because the essence of good manners is that we anticipate the needs of others (though we do need to encourage the reverse procedure by saying some-times, 'Tom hasn't got any jam left, can you pass him some?') Most difficult of all for a child we say, 'You've got to eat a little, even if it's only a spoonful.' Have we always been willing to try snails, eels, frogs' legs, octopus? And how many times have we refused saying, 'No, I don't fancy it/like the look of it?' One mother vividly recalled her 8-year-old daughter offering her some of a poisonous-looking green sweet she had bought with her pocket money. She said, 'No, thank you', her daughter pleaded, 'Go on! it's lovely . . .', and continued to coax. She became angry and snapped, 'I've said I don't want it – now leave me alone.' Whereupon her husband's quiet voice said, 'Shouldn't you try one spoonful? You've always insisted that she did.'

In short, we often expect too much of children too soon, sometimes without setting the example by which they really learn.

Early in life the giving and receiving of food and love are bound up together, and this experience remains very much a part of all our lives. When children begin to learn to feed themselves, however messy and clumsy they are, it is import-ant to them that they still sense love and approval rather than impatience or revulsion.

Sometimes food will be rejected because it is not liked, or it is unfamiliar, or they are not hungry, or because it is just one of those days, and then it is mum who feels rejected! When emotions run high it doesn't take long for mealtimes to become a battleground for a clash of wills. And that's a game nobody wins.

If the good example is there as the background to be absorbed and copied over the years, then parents can afford to give children all the time they need to acquire the *habit* of enjoying food, the *skill* to feed themselves, and the gradual *familiarity* with different smells, tastes and 'feels' of new foods.

When all this is established, then polish can be added to performance.

THE OCCASIONAL VALUE OF SHOCK TACTICS

Just occasionally a short sharp shock can be highly effective. I remember changing schools at 14, going from a school where I was in the lacrosse team to one where they played hockey. I hated being parted from my friends, I was very behind in French and dreaded the lessons, I cringed under a sarcastic teacher, and the one place where I could have shone, on the playing field, was a disaster. Typically, I moaned and grumbled, told everybody what a stupid game hockey was – all those people crouched down over their sticks chasing a stupid ball, instead of leaping into the air to catch and throw. On and on I went, until one day the games mistress drew me aside as we walked off the field and said, 'Now listen. We've done our best to be understanding, and to make allowances for you. But now we're all sick and tired of your constant moaning. We don't play lacrosse. We do play hockey. And you're here. So why not make the best of it?' And with that she walked on, leaving me in a state of shock. Not anger, or fear, or resentment – just shock. I suddenly saw that what she said was true. And it is the truth which sets us free, if only we can let it.

I was lucky, the timing was right and therefore I was able to let it sink in instead of drawing back or lashing out. The next day we had dancing, and she praised me at one point which gave me the courage to say hastily on the way out, 'I'm sorry. I'll put my back into it now and try to make the second eleven.' And she built on it by seeking me out in the shower room to say, 'That was a very pleasant surprise – and I think you'll make it.' I did, and because it was one of the turning points in my life I have never forgotten it.

A mother once told me about her experience with a dearly loved daughter who was coming through a period of depression. Both doctor and family had been concerned and supportive, and no one had used the pointless words 'pull yourself together'. Then one day the mother was driving her daughter somewhere, trying to be the ideal companion, chatting easily but not too brightly, allowing silences but not too long. All to no avail. And suddenly, out of the blue, she heard herself saying firmly, 'I've done all I can do. Nothing makes the slightest difference to you. So now I'm just going to drive and think my own thoughts.' There was a shockwave of silence, and then a relieved voice said, '*Thank* you – I suddenly feel pulled-together – I wish you'd done that weeks ago.' In retrospect the mother was fairly sure it wouldn't have worked 'weeks ago', because she wouldn't have been ready to say it spontaneously, or her daughter to receive it.

Another friend of mine was in a railway carriage recently where a young man ate his way through two tubes of wrapped sweets, and threw every paper on the floor. Everyone in the carriage was aware of it, and exuded disapproval, which went unnoticed. Margaret sat making a conscious effort to find the moral courage to say or do something and finally, just before her station, she bent and picked them all up saying, '*I'll* do it for you this time. It's a pity to discourage the staff who do their best to make the trains clean for us.' Whether or not the shock (and he was shocked) achieved anything no one will know, but at least he was offered an opportunity to pull himself up. But a woman opposite lowered her paper and said with relief, 'I'm so glad you did that. I've been sitting here wondering what to say.' Next time she finds herself in a similar position she may be able to administer her own brand of shock treatment to someone whose behaviour offends.

On another occasion I stood in a crowded train corridor listening to a man swanking to his friend about his dare-devil driving, referring at one point to 'the fun of roaring through country lanes and making the yokels leap into the hedges and ditches'. As the train reached its destination a woman said for all to hear, 'When you have an accident – and of course it is "when" and not "if" – I hope it is you who is killed, or maimed for life, and not an innocent person quietly going about his own life.' He turned bright scarlet – so did the man who had been listening to him without offering his thoughts or reactions to the bragging.

We are all offenders at some time or other, and a short sharp shock can be invaluable. After that it's up to us.

ALLOWING ANGER ITS RIGHTFUL PLACE

One of the most difficult things to learn in life is the difference between temper and anger. Tempers fray when people of any age are tired, worried, out of sorts, or tried beyond endurance by incessant demands made upon them.

When the final provocation comes there are raised voices, slammed doors, a sharp slap perhaps, and things said that aren't meant, or that are meant and should have been said long before, if only it had been possible to communicate.

Occasional loss of temper is a natural release, and allows others to know when they have exceeded permitted limits.

If parents never lose their tempers children can feel guilty about losing their own, and a cycle of repressing natural emotions may begin all over again. Strong feelings need to be experienced and expressed, and lived through, and learned through – not bottled up, for then they so often lead to chronic tiredness or depression.

On the other hand loss of temper can become a habit, and children may suffer more than is realized. Sensitive children may withdraw into themselves and become apathetic. They would rather do nothing than risk doing something 'wrong' that causes an explosion they can't face.

Others who are more resilient may become hardened to the point of saying, 'Go on, hit me! I don't care. It doesn't hurt.'

If things have reached this point do seek help from your doctor or clinic, or someone who understands you and children well enough to know that this isn't anyone's 'fault'. Parents and children are so closely bound up with each other that it is difficult to stand back and see what is happening.

Or try joining a Mother and Toddler group; friendship with others who have been through it all before you can work wonders.

But anger is different. Anger is our response to injustice (as we see it), and has little or nothing to do with our state of mind at the time. Parents try very hard to be fair with their children, and most children therefore grow up with a strong sense of justice. And when they are angry at injustice they often hit out, and there are times when we should respect their feelings rather than censure them or brush them aside.

From a child's point of view it is 'unjust' when a real concentrated effort to achieve something doesn't bring success, and instead of, 'Now, now, temper, temper!' it is more appropriate to say, 'No wonder you are angry, so should I be if I had tried as hard as that and it wouldn't come right. Let's see if we can do it together.'

It is 'unjust' when another child is allowed to barge in and grab what is being played with. Instead of, 'Let her have it, she's only a baby,' it is more appropriate to restore the toy and remove the offender saying, 'No, you can't have that, it is John's, and he's playing with it. Let's find something else.' Personal property should be respected at all times, and only offered to someone else if permission has been asked and *freely* given.

If a child comes home from school complaining angrily about the 'unfairness' of a teacher, listen with an open mind for it may be true. When the anger is spent, sympathize, and work out together how such a situation might be avoided or managed next time.

Children need our help in distinguishing temper from anger. Temper will die down. Anger should be treated with respect, lest it, too, dies down to become apathy or moral cowardice. If we lose our capacity for righteous anger, how shall injustices be brought to light, and wrongs righted?

TO SMACK OR NOT TO SMACK

One of the questions I am asked most often is whether or not children should be smacked. There are some parents who reject the idea absolutely because they see it as an infringement of human rights and dignity, or as a sign of weakness and lack of self-control, or because it sets a bad example. Others think it isn't necessary, given patience and understanding.

Some don't have moral objections to smacking, but say 'I couldn't do it, I should feel so awful afterwards.' When asked why, two fundamental fears are usually revealed, fear of feeling guilty, and fear of damaging the relationship.

Guilt at smacking often springs from the feeling that parents should be perfect – always loving, patient, reasonable and long-suffering. But that is a disastrous picture of perfection, all too often leading to nervous exhaustion or bouts of quite deep depression. It can also set up the same guilt cycle in the child, as some of us may remember from our own childhood.

Since our parents are perfect (so our infantile reasoning went), then I must be horrid and unworthy if I can't live up to that standard; worse still, if the loved parent cries, or falls ill and has to retire to bed, it must be my fault. Once children start to blame themselves for causing illness or unhappiness, then they strive harder to please – and life becomes one long struggle to make everybody happy.

There are also parents who smack constantly, knowing that they shouldn't but unable to stop themselves. This pattern can begin in the first year, especially if the parents have had nothing to do with children in their lives before. Unrealistic expectations of their baby's behaviour undermines confidence, and life can become one long clash of needs. A slap is often a cry for help from the parent to the baby, '*Please* keep still . . . stop kicking . . . I can't get your nappy on . . . I'm doing my best . . .' The cycle of wanting, trying, asking, shouting and slapping can become a habit if help isn't forthcoming.

Fewer parents these days resort to the unfair, 'Wait until your father comes home . . .' This is always unsatisfactory, partly because the time lag between the misdemeanour and the punishment is too long, but mostly because the mother loses the child's respect by not being able to deal with whatever-it-was on the spot. The father is also put in the position of having to punish something he hasn't witnessed without being able to judge for himself the rights and wrongs of the original situation.

The real test of whether or not smacking 'works' may lie with those adults who can recall how they felt about it when they were children. According to these recollections gleaned over the years it seems that children would rather be smacked occasionally than have to endure 'atmospheres', or the guilt induced by the spoken or unspoken message, 'Your lack of consideration has made me ill.'

On the other hand they grow hardened and indifferent to perpetual nagging and slapping. Sometimes they repeat the pattern with their own children. Sometimes they avoid it like the plague. Which they do seems to depend on whether or not they felt love behind the exhaustion and exasperation. If they did, all is well in later years. If they didn't, problems are apt to carry over into the next generation when the parents become grandparents.

Human dignity was indeed infringed for those who remember being put across a bed, or knee, or having knickers or pants removed, before being smacked.

The happiest childhoods seem to coincide with memories of the *very occasional*, well-deserved, sharp slap administered spontaneously in the heat of the moment. Because of its honesty and immediacy it was effective in stopping whatever was going on, and was usually followed by a cooling-off period before overtures of friendship were offered and accepted on both sides.

What is also remembered is that some of these incidents were over and done with without further reference, but that on other occasions there were explanations that helped to clear the air – with apologies offered (not asked for) by one, other, or both, as appropriate. Parents recalled that they liked the 'over and done with' approach to things they knew they shouldn't have done, but were grateful for the subsequent explanations of those misdemeanours which had deeper significance, or greater repercussions, than they realized at the time.

IDENTIFYING THE CAUSES OF AGGRESSION

Temper tantrums are up-and-over affairs. The cause is usually frustration at not being able to do what the child wants to do, either because a task is beyond their abilities, or because they are forbidden to do or have what they want to do or have.

This is a healthy sign of growing up. It is a way of saying 'I've just discovered that you are you, and I am me. I thought we were a horse and cart, with me always having to go where you led. But I can go by myself . . .'

The time has come to give them more independence, but inevitably there will be times when frustration builds up and erupts in explosive release.

Aggression is rather different. Some children are just naturally more assertive and aggressive than others, girls as well as boys. Their sense of 'self' is very strong, and it is quite difficult to bring them up in such a way that they are neither crushed nor allowed to become bullies. If the happy medium is found they often become sturdy individualists and pillars of strength, fighting for truth and justice where once they fought for themselves (or for the sake of fighting).

Other children become aggressive in a group. There may be two very innocent reasons for this. An only child, or a child from a quiet home, may become uncontrollably excited, rather like some people at a buffet, when the table spread with tempting dishes in profusion leads them to throw their usual good manners overboard as they pile their plates high and push their way back for more.

Or they may long to play and simply not have the social skills to enter into a play partnership. Rather than reprimanding the pusher and grabber put an arm round him or her and try, 'You want a ride very badly, don't you? Let's ask Andrew to give it to you when he's finished.'

Sometimes children come from a family where the older ones tend to push them about a bit, and when they get with children of their own age they wade in with the determination that if anyone gets pushed around it's not going to be them this time.

The nearest adult can intervene right at the beginning to say, 'It's all right, no one is going to hurt you here. We all help each other,' and then make sure that this proves to be true.

If the aggression is longstanding, and the child doesn't seem to be a happy individualist, then it may be for one of two reasons: they feel insufficiently loved, or insufficiently controlled.

At any age love and respect have to go together. A child can't trust a love that doesn't know how, when or where to set limits. Or feel secure if limits are set without love. And some parents find it particularly difficult to set limits with loving firmness.

Parents who lacked love in their own childhood, or who grew up with too little confidence in themselves, are often frightened of losing the love of their children. Their 'No' holds good for a while, and then tears melt their resolve. Or they can withstand tears, but not the hurt of 'I hate you, I hate you, I wish you were dead!' Yet that is the ultimate compliment; it says, 'I dare to say the worst thing in the world in the heat of the moment, because I know that even then you won't stop loving me.' That's love, not hate.

Never say 'No' unless you mean it. But when you do, stand by it. Holding firm will exhaust you at first, but growing confidence and self-respect will make it all worthwhile.

UNDERSTANDING FEAR OF THE DARK

Children are not born with a fear of the dark, but like any other fear it can be acquired quickly. If a baby is habitually left to cry alone at night, then gradually a connection is made between darkness, hunger, pain and loneliness. The memory of the distress can linger on long after a regular sleeping habit is established, and the occasional waking in the night – especially after a bad dream – may bring it back and trigger more fear. Comfort and reassurance is the quickest way of breaking these old associations.

The fear of loud noises *is* one that we are born with, and darkness can intensify this instinctive reaction: the sharp crack of contracting or expanding metal as radiators cut in or out, cats wailing under the window, a car backfiring, high wind or thunder can all be genuinely frightening.

The unknown also holds fear, especially in the dark when the cause can't be identified. A street light, or the moon shining through curtains, especially if a draught blows them, can make dark shadows move across the walls and ceiling almost as though they are alive. Alone in the darkness such shadows can be frightening, whereas in daylight we are almost always in the presence of shadows that go unnoticed. Explain what is happening.

Then there comes the stage when children begin to realize how big the world is, and how small and dependent they are on the love and protection of their parents. Fear of losing their protectors can be intense at times, and if they wake to silence and darkness the irrational fear 'I can't see or hear them – they must have gone', can flash into their minds. I can remember saying 'Leave the landing light on – and make a noise downstairs.' And they did, and I felt safe.

We can also convey fear to children unintentionally, 'No, it's dark in there . . . come on!', or 'It's all dark out there, shut the door, quick!'

All these and other experiences build up fear of the dark, just as other experiences build up pleasure.

Fears can't be overcome by discipline, impatience, teasing or exhortation. They have to be outgrown, and the surest way is through a reassuring build up of confidence. And if the presence of a landing light brings comfort, then leave it on until the need for it is outgrown.

PART THREE

ENCOURAGING CHILDREN TO BE CONFIDENT AND RESPONSIBLE

CARRYING MESSAGES

We make a valuable contribution to children's learning if we can help them to carry messages accurately. This is a skill we take for granted, but it is much more difficult for young children than we realize.

Usually we speak to children directly, 'Put it on . . . eat it up . . . give it to me . . . don't touch . . . look at this!' Or we ask them questions which they answer then and there. Or we refer to something in the past, and they recall as much as they can in their own words. But it requires concentration and practice to be able to take in a message, walk away from us to a different person in a different place, and then to remember and repeat the exact words.

Like any new skill it is best learned together, 'Let's go and tell them that dinner's ready!' and off you go together to impart the news, and bring them back for handwashing while the meal is dished up. Once the ritual is established children can be relied upon to 'Go and tell them dinner's ready', but any variation may prove difficult – so don't expect accuracy first time if you say 'Tell them dinner will be ready in half an hour, and when they come in will they please bring some fresh mint.'

Children may try to remember a message by heart, but they will be in danger of forgetting or muddling it if something distracts their attention on the way. They are much more likely to remember if they understand what is happening, and why a message is necessary, 'I think my watch has stopped, can you hear it ticking? No? Neither can I. I wonder what the time is? Could you go and ask Grandad what his watch says?' The chances are the child will understand this well enough not only to ask Grandad but to listen to his watch as well, and to return with the information.

When understanding is incomplete some very strange messages can be relayed. Our 6-year-old came home from school one day bursting with the urgent news that we must be sure to save all our silver milk tops, 'Because Helen's Aunty's blind dog needs them very badly.'

LEARNING TO MAKE DECISIONS TOGETHER

Many of us probably wish we had the opportunity and courage to make a few more decisions according to what we really want to do, rather than in accordance with what we were brought up to think we ought to do – or else in defiance of our upbringing.

A group of us was talking about this one day when someone said, 'I've just seen something! My mother never allowed any of us to eat in the street because it wasn't lady-like. And now that I've got children I'm getting my own back. I can never pass a baker's shop without going in and buying us all doughnuts. I deliberately buy the messiest things I can, and we come out eating them, and getting jam and sugar all over us. I've seen something else, too. I'm a twin but my sister still can't bring herself to eat in the street, or to allow her children to. Neither of us has made a really free decision – I've rebelled and she's conformed. We haven't decided for ourselves, for our own reasons.'

Even when we think we really are making sound and rational decisions we often delude ourselves. We may decide we need a new three-piece suite because ours is worn, or too small, or too large, or uncomfortable, and the decision may be wise. But on the other hand the truth may be that we feel left out of things compared to our friends, and hope a new look to our home will give the much needed lift to our spirits.

We may decide not to complain to the cleaners about a badly pressed coat because 'it wasn't worth it', or we 'didn't want to make a fuss', whereas the truth may be that we lack the confidence to complain (even though it is justified).

Even when we are used to making decisions, and accepting responsibility for them, it can still be a tiring business. Most of us feel the need to opt out occasionally, saying 'What shall we have to eat at the weekend?' or 'Shall I wear this or that?'

Many decisions are a matter of convenience (fish on the day the van comes round the villages). Or because we want a change (blue emulsion paint last time, a floral wallpaper this time). Or for financial considerations (we can't afford a holiday, we'll have days out).

More complicated decisions need to be talked through many times, first highlighting all the advantages, then the disadvantages to the family as a whole – then again on behalf of each individual member. And then it takes time for all the facts and feelings to simmer in the deep recesses of our minds until the moment is reached when the decision resolves itself – not just the 'Yes' or 'No' at the end of a balance sheet of pros and cons, but the moment of 'knowing'. Act on that moment, and agree that if it should prove to be wrong in the light of later experience, you will neither blame yourselves nor each other. Just let it go, and chalk it up to experience.

Understand your own decision-making processes, and then begin to help your children to make decisions. They, too, find it frustrating to have all their decisions made for them, and tire of making too many. Be understanding when they rationalize, sometimes accepting their need and sometimes helping them to get to the underlying reason. And when they make a wrong decision *never* say 'I told you so!' Back them, and help them to chalk it up to experience in their turn.

THE DISCIPLINE OF IF, THEN AND THEREFORE

Children find it so difficult to remember all that we tell them, partly because we are so often negative instead of positive, and partly because they have to try to 'remember' since we don't always take the time to explain things in such a way that they 'know'.

If we put ourselves in their place we can understand how much more effective positive advice is than negative criticism. 'Please keep the drive-way clear' disposes us to be co-operative. 'Parking prohibited' or 'No Parking' still elicits response in most of us, if less willingly. But 'Doctor's garage. Please keep clear at all times' has us eager to comply – we all want our doctors to be able to get to us in an emergency. We understand. We don't feel we're being bossed around.

So it is with children. 'Look at you, you're soaking' is a reprimand that comes too late to do any good – and it may put the child off playing at the sink again. And if it does we are both losers; the child misses out on the sort of play that is so valuable, and we will be hard put to it to find a toy that offers the long-shared peace of being alongside a child totally absorbed in water play. What is more, a child who comes down to earth after being lost to the world in this kind of play, is peaceful and fulfilled; a child who is constantly told not to do this and that becomes frustrated or apathetic – which has its repercussions on our nervous system as well as their personalities.

This doesn't mean I am advocating that children should do just what they like, when they like, how they like. It just means that anticipation on our part, and the ability to acquire the knack of thinking of the consequences in terms of If, Then and Therefore, is a form of self-discipline that pays tremendous dividends.

We are all caught out the first time our children do something. If it's the first tooth, or the first step, we are delighted beyond all reason – mothers have even been known to phone fathers at work to share the excitement. If it's the first wet, messy or broken disaster, then we are apt to go equally overboard in anger or distress. That's fair enough. But our first shock reaction doesn't have to be the one that sets the pattern of response to all the misdemeanours that follow (the majority of which are due to innocent ignorance or accident). If you find you are consistently snapping, then perhaps you should go and see your doctor; it is distressing for you to live with frayed nerves, and it does more harm to your children than you may foresee.

Parents are the most important and influential people in a child's life, and that first relationship sets the pattern for all those that follow; this is why that first relationship needs to be one of love, trust, confidence and hope.

The greatest block to learning isn't lack of intelligence, it is intelligence dammed up by fear. Many a child can't 'try harder' at school because, at a subconscious level, something is saying, 'IF I get it wrong, THEN the teacher may be cross, THEREFORE it would be safest not to commit myself to paper, or to answering in class.' Such a child has often learned that anything which displeases parents has distressing emotional consequences – to be wet, dirty, noisy, clumsy, cross, upset, above all 'wrong', is to lose love and esteem. Consequently they tend to grow up with so little confidence and self-esteem that much of their energy goes into trying to be good enough to earn love – and they see goodness as absence of badness.

Goodness has to be more than that! It is to dare to live fully, even though that will inevitably lead to mistakes and suffering, but supported by love, all those mistakes and all that suffering will be ploughed-in to become the enriched ground of personality upon which the next stage of learning will be based.

I have yet to meet the parent who didn't love his or her children, and who didn't try to be a responsible parent. But some parents are handicapped by negative memories of being dominated or 'downed'. Never mind, there's nothing to stop us saying to ourselves, 'IF I endlessly say "don't", THEN my children will lose confidence in their worth and ability, THEREFORE I will try to cut the word right out of my vocabulary except as a last resort.' Try it, and keep a score of the 'don'ts' you nearly said; one mother clocked up 27 before lunch.

Instead of, 'Don't spill it', try 'Slowly!': instead of 'Don't run', try 'Isn't it slippery? We shall have to walk carefully'; instead of 'Don't put so much in your mouth', try 'If you put smaller pieces in your mouth you will taste them better'; instead of 'Don't make that noise', either suggest making it somewhere else, or offer a tupperware lidded basin with a wooden spoon instead of a tin drum; instead of 'That was naughty' wait until you can say 'That was kind and helpful, thank you.'

Learn, too, to anticipate trouble, and plan to avoid it. If your child has reached the stage of being addicted to water say to yourself, '*If* water is played with, *then* inevitably some will be spilt, *therefore* I must make or buy a waterproof apron and floor covering, and get a small pail and child's-hand sized cloth for mopping up.' Then next time you see someone making a beeline for the sink you can say, 'Are you going to play with water? Let's just cover the floor, and put your apron on.' And before the inevitable if accidental splashes get out of hand you can move in with, 'Just a minute, let's just mop up the spills before it gets too wet – here's your bucket and cloth and I'll show you how we do it – or can you remember how to do it?

Children become what we presume them to be. If we presume they are going to be difficult or a nuisance, then that is what they will become, therefore we need to plan for, look for, and reinforce the good in all that they say, and do, and are.

ALLOWING CHILDREN TO GROW UP

Back in the early summer I met a mother who has stayed in my mind. She had just seen her daughter – we'll call her Ruth – off on a hiking weekend, and felt 'awful . . . guilty and anxious'.

In spite of all suggestions Ruth had elected to set off in the shortest of shorts, t-shirt, windcheater and 'unsuitable' shoes. The weather was cold, the forecast worse, and this 'wisp of a thing who felt the cold at the best of times' refused to weigh herself down with any extras.

Both parents were happy about her companions, and although the thought of blistered feet, windchapped legs and exhaustion were real enough, Ruth's mother felt they would all look after each other. But that wasn't what troubled her, the real dilemma lay deeper.

At the eleventh hour it was fairly apparent that Ruth didn't want to go, neither did she want to cry off, and it seemed likely that she might (without realizing it) have opted for an alternative way out – by trying to provoke her mother into preventing it. Was she, just possibly, trying to goad her mother into saying, 'Well, you're not going in those inadequate shoes and shorts, and I'm not going to nurse you if you get pneumonia, so either you go upstairs and get suitably dressed or you don't go at all'?

If so, then the reply could have been, 'I'm not going to change . . . you're treating me like a child . . . so I shan't go then!' At this point she would have been let off the hook, and could have saved face with her friends by slamming out of the house to find a phone, and ringing one to say, 'Mum won't let me go. I'm all dressed and packed and ready, and suddenly she's put her foot down.'

Most of us know this conversation; I had it with my mother, and my daughter had it with me. In both cases we had asked permission to go to London alone with a special friend; in both cases the idea secretly terrified us, but we didn't want to appear cowardly; in both cases we were overwhelmingly relieved when we weren't allowed to go, but said to our friends, 'She won't let me . . . I knew she wouldn't. She always spoils everything,' and in both cases we later confessed our disloyalty, to be told, 'It's all right. That's what parents are for sometimes.'

So they are – up to a point. But there comes a time when we all have to find the moral courage to extricate ourselves from tight corners without relying on someone to do it for us. This takes so much courage that it can't be taken for granted without a period of preparation and help.

On this particular occasion the mother sensed what was happening, and felt instinctively that it was a game neither of them should be playing. She climbed down gracefully and said, 'You're quite right, I'm behaving like a fussy mother! You young ones don't feel the cold like I do. Off you go then, and have a lovely time.' She deliberately made the atmosphere loving so that it wouldn't be too difficult for Ruth to say either, 'Well, I'll put on jeans and a jumper if it will make you any happier,' or 'I don't much want to go . . .'. But after a slightly stricken look, and a spontaneous hug, Ruth set off, with her mother calling out, 'I'll have a hot bath and a good hot meal waiting for you when you get back!'

I wish I knew the end of the story. Ruth will undoubtedly have learned from firsthand experience, together with her observation of others, what to wear and carry on her next hike – if, indeed, she wants to hike again. But at least she knows what it's all about now. And if she didn't suffer too much she will also have come through with increased self-confidence.

Her mother will be glad that even though her advice was rejected, she didn't withhold her love and encouragement. This 'permission' to go forth without guilt, anxiety or fear frees our children to take up a challenge with good heart and confidence, while also leaving them free to come back for comfort and encouragement if need be.

Next time, Ruth's mother may be able to say, 'Look, I may be quite wrong, but I've got a feeling you don't really want to do this, and that you're hoping I will get you out of it. Let's just sit down and talk about it. Something's bothering you isn't it? Tell me about it.' And then she will *listen*, and help Ruth to work out her solution.

HELPING CHILDREN WHO CAN'T GET UP IN THE MORNING

We all have our own differing needs for sleep, and our own pattern, some of us are at our best in the morning, and others really don't come to life until the evening. Within limits this has to be accepted, but we all still have to meet the demands of the clock at certain points.

One of the difficult times of day is the early morning rush hour in the house. Members of the family queue up for the bathroom. Work, school and playgroup mean people have different deadlines. Some have different breakfast needs. One may find it nearly impossible to come to the surface at all.

Those of you who have one of these children know the drill only too well. You wake them, draw the curtains, talk gently but firmly until wakefulness seems assured, and then depart. Ten minutes later you go back to find a hump in the bed, which indicates that your offspring has burrowed away from the light and returned to sleep. You strip the bedclothes off and use a firmer voice, perhaps even a pat on the shoulder or a bodily lifting to a sitting position, and the refrain begins: 'Come on . . . wake up . . . it's getting late . . .' The sleepy head staggers off to the bathroom and you dash down to cope with everybody else.

Nothing happens; it's all gone quiet upstairs. You start again, 'Breakfast! Come on, hurry up, it's getting late.' Silence.

You go up to find him or her sitting dreamily on the floor, half dressed, trying to make a garage for a small car out of a shoe turned on its side, or experimenting to see if the face flannel would act as well as a plug in the basin.

According to the day and your mood you either start to get distinctly irritable, or you say, 'Come on love, I'll help. Here, head through . . .'

And then it begins all over again downstairs. I remember one such breakfast when, having seen my husband off and washed the marmalade from our daughter's hands and face, I returned to find our son carefully sticking large toast crumbs end-up in the butter. When I said, 'What on earth are you doing?' he replied, 'Those are my bantams.'

With us this daily pattern went on and on. I repeated the same rituals each morning, and without even being aware of it I went on saying the same things again and again, like a worn-out gramophone record.

And then one day (our son was 8 by then) I suddenly woke up to what was happening. He was *waiting* for me to go through my performance, I had conditioned him to the endlessly repeated sequence of events. Somehow we had to break the pattern.

One evening when we were thoroughly switched on to each other, I explained how much I hated being worried and impatient every morning, and said that I had decided to call him only once in future, starting from tomorrow. We went through it quite carefully together. One good rousing call to be sure that he really was awake, and then he would have to get himself to the bathroom, get dressed, eat breakfast and go off to school without any help from me at all.

I duly woke him, reminded him of our plan, and went downstairs. At 9.15 am he came down to breakfast, which I gave him in very friendly fashion, and at 9.45 am he suddenly came to and said in a panic, 'I shall be late for school!' I agreed that he would. He was quite white with shock, and said hopefully, 'Will you write a note?' I said that I wouldn't, but that we would talk through together what he could do when he got to school: slip in late, lurk in the cloakroom until a lesson change or playtime, or go straight to the master and say 'I'm sorry I'm late.' He chose the latter of course and stuck to it. Seeing him off was terrible! He looked so small and vulnerable, and had such courage. I called out, 'It will be all right – and you can have *two* poached eggs on toast for tea!' It was all right, and he was never late again.

The episode taught me a lesson: if children aren't faced with the natural consequence of their actions (because we prevent it by taking the responsibility upon ourselves), then they can't learn. It is so unfair to blame and nag them for an impossible situation at which we have connived.

UNDERSTANDING THE POSITIVE ASPECT OF AGGRESSION

Aggressive children and teenagers cause so much disturbance in the family and the community, that we may be in danger of overlooking those at the opposite end of the scale, the too-good children who cause no trouble to anyone, but could be laying trouble for themselves in later life.

The children who should concern us are not the naturally quiet or the sunny-natured children, but those who are 'good' for fear of being 'bad'; this may be convenient for parents and teachers, but it isn't healthy.

If the fear is due to physical or emotional cruelty – such as frequent punishment, or threats of 'I'll send you away . . .', or 'I'll go away and never come back . . .' – then this is so obviously damaging that it needs no further explanation.

The less obvious fear of being bad is rooted in guilt and fear. If dearly loved parents can't accept bad behaviour sometimes as a natural part of growing up, but become upset or up-tight, then the child tries to repress it in order to please. The message received is, 'Be good, and I'll love you, and you will be safe. Be bad, and you'll upset me, and your punish-ment will be that love is withdrawn, and then you won't be safe.' This is emotional blackmail, though blame is pointless, for most of the parents concerned are unaware of what they are doing. But the need to please everybody, always, is a strain no one should carry into adult life.

Sometimes the guilt is caused by parents being over-protective. They are afraid of their child catching cold, getting overtired, being bullied, being hurt, or being exposed to any kind of known or imagined danger, and this constant cau-tioning and background anxiety can lead to children losing confidence in their own judgement. There was quite a lot of this kind of guilt in my own childhood; I was particularly close to my mother, and it was extremely hard to go against her ideas of what *she* thought would be best for *me*.

I remember at the age of 22 (for heaven's sake!) preparing to go to London to meet my soldier husband for 48 hours leave, and mother saying, 'Darling, you shouldn't go with a cold like that, phone and ask him to come here . . .' I insisted on going, but I can still remember the flood of relief when she changed her mind and said, 'Of course! You're a married woman now, bless you – go and have a lovely time.'

But I shouldn't have needed 'permission' before I could go with a light heart, or been deterred by the background guilt of, 'If I get pneumonia it will be my fault, and she's the one who will have to nurse me.' This wasn't just common to my generation, the country is full of people, of both sexes and all ages, who still need spoken or unspoken 'permission' before they can accept responsibility for their own thoughts, feelings and actions. We all welcome approval, but we shouldn't constantly *need* it.

If children are smother-loved, over-protected, over-indulged materially and emotionally, and gentled out of all aggressive behaviour, then they are being damaged. Positive aggression, that is the life-force which should be thrusting them out into the world with a zest for living, is being eroded.

Fortunately for us all nature is very persistent, and usually guides children subconsciously to release their aggression through play. It may be running, chasing, shouting and the kicking of balls round the playground. Or it may be through the make believe of cops and robbers, where it is 'all right' to shout, chase, capture or kill the baddies, and sometimes the symbolic 'killing' of the baddy is the child's only safe way of 'killing' the repressive ban on his or her natural aggression. It is not only safe but therapeutic, and if it is played-out it is highly unlikely to be acted-out for real later.

Older children will sometimes find release in amateur dramatics, and it is amazing how violent and vicious an unnaturally 'good' person can be in the portrayal of tyrants, thugs and murderers.

Many years ago I remember two teenage brothers who used to play for hours in their back garden, dressed up in Nazi uniforms, barking orders, drilling and charging imaginary foes. The uniforms gave them 'permission' to release feelings and tones of voice which wouldn't have been acceptable to their parents in their own *persona*. But there are the seeds of danger here. If the only way children and teenagers can release their aggression is in the character of someone else, then there is a splitting-off of part of the personality which should be integrated.

We should be able to release honest anger immediately it is raised, and in proportion to what has caused it – if we can't it either goes underground and robs us of our energy, or it is stored up ready to burst out of all proportion, or it's dissipated in nasty under-cover little ways. Don't expect or want your children to be too good.

CONSULTATION AND COMPROMISE

Part of a parent's role is to encourage their children to make choices and decisions – but choice and decision without the chance of prior consultation may lead to some very prickly confrontations.

The buying and wearing of clothes can become decidedly fraught if children and young people are either given no choice, or a free choice. I remember a teenager telling how she saved up for a dress for special dates, and asked her mother to go shopping with her. She couldn't afford the dress they both liked best, but was settling very happily for the one she could afford when Mum came to the rescue, saying 'Go on! Have the one you love, and I'll pay the difference.' Saturday evening came, and after hours spent in preparation Sue – feeling wonderful – came downstairs to show herself off. She was greeted with 'And where do you think you're going in that dress?', to which the answer was 'Brian's birthday party'. Her mother then said, 'Well, you can just go upstairs and take it off, I bought that for you to wear with us, not for going around with the crowd.' Sue said, 'But you didn't buy it, you helped *me* to buy it – and this was what I wanted it for,' and there followed an angry and tearful exchange, with both sides feeling let down and bitter.

Standing in the fitting room the comparisons and choice of dress, by reflection in the mirror, had been easy. The decision on price had been made on the strength of the spontaneous gift. But there had been no consultation on the occasion for which it was intended, or on whether the extra money was a free gift or had strings attached.

From the earliest years we need to share preliminary thinking with our children. If we already think-through silently it just means learning to do it aloud, but if we tend to be impulse buyers, then the mental discipline is likely to be as helpful for us as our children. It means being specific, 'You need some new playclothes,' or 'Let's go and find a pretty dress to wear for Christmas.' It also means allowing time for the idea to sink in, and for the pleasure of anticipation to be aroused – saying it in the bus on the way into town is too rushed.

Once in the right section of the shop we need to share our thoughts, 'Do you like this? . . . that's too expensive . . . that won't let down . . . yes, that would do . . . and that. Let's go and try these on.' Having then set the permitted limits within which choice can be made, the trying-on stage calls for real consultation, 'Can you bend down . . . lift your arms . . . sit comfortably?'

After uncomfortable clothes have been eliminated it is valuable for the child's esteem for him or her to make the final choice, and to have that decision ratified by our warm approval – even if we prefer the one that got away.

LESSENING THE TENSION OF BUYING SHOES

As any parent knows, buying shoes for children can be difficult. We all want to be wise, and try to budget for good well-fitting shoes the minute the old ones are outgrown. But when it comes to the actual buying children can be less than co-operative.

Sometimes younger children scream and refuse to allow their own shoes to be removed. This can be a way of saying 'What are you doing to me? Undressing me? Are you going to leave me here?' They need preparation for the event if they are not to feel anxious. Look at the old shoes together, and talk about buying new ones for a few days before it happens. And once in the shop if the removal of shoes still seems likely to cause distress, slip your own off first. This is the equivalent of saying 'It's all right. I shan't go and leave you because I haven't got any shoes on either.'

The other major problem is style. I remembr a fraught bedtime when our son said 'You can buy beetle-squashers if you like – but I shan't wear them. I want pointed toes like everyone else.' I also remember a nasty moment in the middle of the night when the still small voice of my conscience said, 'You don't care nearly as much about his feet as you do about proving that you are still top-dog now that he's taller than you.'

And that was true, too.

In the morning we compromised. He put his foot on a sheet of thick paper, I drew round it, and he cut it out and put it in his pocket. We agreed that he could have pointed shoes *if* we could find a pair that didn't distort the paper pattern when it was matched to the sole of the shoe.

The exercise was instructive for both of us, and eventually we found a pair which were wide enough where it mattered before they tapered to the prized point.

They cost the shoe-money, plus much of the housekeeping – but it was the best money we spent that year. He loved and polished those shoes as though they were the crown jewels, and his gratitude and joy were more than compensation for the soup, baked beans, potatoes in their jackets, cheese and bread which were our staple diet that week.

Try all the available shops until you find something that satisfies you both. It is worth the effort. You are not just buying shoes, you are both learning about responsibility and the give and take of honest compromise.

ACCEPTING CHILDREN'S CONTRIBUTIONS TO THE FAMILY AT THEIR OWN LEVEL

One day during the off-peak holiday season I travelled on a long-distance train packed with holidaymakers. The atmosphere was reminiscent of the last day of term. Everyone was in bubbling high spirits, and the usual reserve had broken down as people shared their destinations with each other. 'Blackpool . . . there's nowhere on earth quite like it!'; 'Kendall, we go back to the Lakes year after year'; 'Carlisle, we've got relations there, you see'; 'Blackpool! We went there as kids, and now we take our kids.'

The happiness was wonderfully contagious, and blurred the edges of the age gap as retired couples identified with parents taking children to visit grandparents, and the younger generation recalled going on holiday with their parents before 'things changed so'.

There they all were – new shoes and sandals, clean socks and dresses, new jumpers and skirts and jeans, best sports jackets and open-necked shirts, whole new co-ordinated outfits, and Sunday suits with collars and ties, heads of shining well-cut hair, newly emerged from the hairdresser or bathroom, raincoats neatly folded on every overhead luggage rack, and luggage of every colour, size and shape under the sun.

At lunchtime different family patterns began to emerge. Some went to the dining car, one elderly couple saying almost apologetically, 'Lunch on the train is our one big holiday extravagance – we love it, eating and watching the scenery go by.' In some families it was always the man who went to the buffet car, coming back with coffee, then later sandwiches or a cooked snack, then back later for plastic beakers of tea. And his wife said 'Thank you, dear' – and meant it.

Sometimes it was bigger children who went, taking younger brothers and sisters to help carry the load. And sometimes it was the mother, still in her role as organiser and provider of meals.

But mostly the preparation of a packed lunch had been part of the planning. Sometimes it was a pile of sandwiches wrapped in foil, sometimes individual packets for each member of the family, sometimes a quiche in the familiar M & S wrapping.

It was at this point that I noticed the mother and two children who will stay in my mind quite possibly for ever. The mother was small, dark and vivacious, the two children were just as vividly alive – a boy of about 8 and a girl perhaps two years younger.

They bubbled and sparked off each other, and there appeared to be no age gap at all, not because the children were precocious, or the mother childish, but because they related to each other as people – as friends. But it was the lunch that first got to me. The boy dived into the plastic carrier bag he had been guarding, and with the flourish and pride of a conjurer he produced the lunch that he had clearly prepared himself.

Somewhat untidy sandwiches emerged, made with sliced bread that hadn't been stuck together quite accurately, so whiskers of cress stuck out, and pieces of hard-boiled egg escaped as they all tucked in. Then came homemade cake that had been cut by pressing-down with a knife rather than sawing, so instead of neat slices there were lumps in a nest of crumbs. They shared the lumps, and then gathered up the crumbs between fingers and thumbs, until finally the boy tipped the last few from the foil into the palms of his mother's and sister's hands.

It was like looking at three lovely children sharing a secret feast – and I wondered why on earth I had always felt it was my job to try and do everything (perfectly) for my children on every possible occasion, instead of allowing them to do it for me sometimes. And if I had, would I have been able to appreciate and enjoy it at their level, without 'helping' to bring it up to my standards? I don't know.

The last I saw of them was a cheerful trio struggling towards the ticket barrier. The youngest child had bulging plastic carrier bags in each hand, stuffed with soft clothing and with a small teddy bear tucked into the top of one. The boy had a bulging featherweight zipped grip in one hand, balanced by a shoulder bag which was causing slight problems. The mother had a bigger grip, clearly with the weight in it, and a holdall-cum-handbag hanging from the other arm leaving one hand free to shepherd the children through the crowd, and to help her son with his slipping load.

I called out, 'They're coping manfully!' and with a lovely twinkle in her eye she replied, 'Womanfully, I think!' and then added, 'We do this trip quite often, and I used to pack, carry and do everything – I got so tired and cross and martyred that the journey was misery for us all. So now we share everything, and we all enjoy it.'

I think we often try too hard to bring children up to our standards, instead of appreciating and enjoying them at the level where they can make a genuine contribution to family life.

PART FOUR

EXPERIENCES AT THE HEART OF CHILDHOOD

MAKING MUD PIES

One of the most nostalgic memories many parents have is of making mud pies, and it would be sad if we became so sophisticated that we felt modelling clay bought from a shop was somehow 'better'.

Since the spores of tetanus, or lockjaw, live in the soil it is wise to have children inoculated against this as a matter of course. Given this protection then mud pies can be thoroughly recommended.

As children we had an old kitchen table cut down to our height, and it lived in the garden as a permanent part of our play. In the mud-pie season we carried buckets of earth to the table, tipped them out, made a well in the centre, and poured in water from golden syrup tins. We stirred and mixed with sticks, patted and shaped with our hands, fetched dry earth from under the hedge if it was too wet, or more water if it was too dry. Then we discovered that if the earth was dry we could sift it just as Mother sifted flour and icing sugar – with the very same sieve! It was given to us, and our play took on a new lease of life. We mixed the sifted earth with water in our syrup tin and made lovely smooth thick paint, and painted the old table with Father's old paint-brushes. Then when it dried we scraped it all off with sticks and started again. Or we scrubbed it off with an old scrubbing brush and a nailbrush, having competitions to see whose half was cleanest. But mostly we just revelled in the feel of it, and there are photographs of us contemplating our long black 'gloves' of mud with deep satisfaction.

As the years went by the play changed again and we made elaborate cakes, with ground blackboard-chalk icing, sawdust chopped nuts and mud pellet chocolate drops.

First we used leaves for plates; then we discovered we could make mud plates and mugs. Mother baked them in the oven, and we painted the ones that survived without breaking. Yellow privet leaves made white bread sandwiches with 'sardine' mud filling. We dished up sausages with chopped grass spinach and white stone potatoes, swimming in rich thick mud gravy. It was bliss.

I am sad for children who miss all this; and for the parents who missed out before them, for you can't hand on what you haven't had, unless you have the chance, and the open mind, to pick up the idea later on. Parents who were brought up to feel guilty every time they were dirty often find it particularly hard to allow messy play. As one mother put it, 'I watch her do things I used to love doing, and I want her to go on enjoying it. But I can hear what my mother used to say to me, and something makes me say it to her even though I don't want to.'

One mother living in a high-rise flat was so determined that her children wouldn't be denied this childhood pleasure that she carried home biscuit tins of earth from her mother's garden. When she had made enough journeys she tipped the earth out on the balcony in a big tray, offered a cooking spoon and a plastic mug of water, and sat back to recapture memories as her child slowly made the same discoveries.

Children can have hours of pleasure if parents find a way to make it possible for them to be messy in peace.

ENJOYING WATER

Whilst swimming in our local pool recently I saw a mother with a beautiful child in her arms, gently bobbing up and down in a brilliantly sunlit patch of water at the shallow end. I watched for some time. They were so completely self-contained and oblivious to the rest of us that we all instinctively kept well away, lest noise and splashes intruded on their contentment.

The mother was trailing one hand through the water, then bringing it up to let the drops slip from her finger tips. The child watched intently, then reached out to catch the shining cascade; the mother lowered herself in the water until the child could also trail her hands and fingers in the water, and she laughed with delight: the mother clasped the child close to her, and dipped and rose rhythmically so that the water slid up and down her body from toes to chin. It was like watching a slow motion picture. Later the mother supported the slippery little body, first back and then front, while she walked slowly through the water, with the child either kicking and splashing in happy excitement, or almost dozing with the gentle lap and rhythm of the water flowing under and round her.

As they prepared to leave the water I swam up to say how much I had enjoyed watching them, and asked if they came often. The mother said that they came to the pool more often than they went in and had a swim, 'If I can see through the glass doors that the pool is noisy and crowded we go away again.' I asked how old her daughter was when she first started, and was told she had been 10 months – and then I heard the full story.

The mother and father couldn't swim. They both wanted to learn themselves, and to see to it that their children learned early, 'It's so much easier to pick things up when you're young, isn't it?' Enquiries revealed that there was a cygnets class each week for babies from a few months old to 2 years. A parent had to be responsible for each child, and in the water with them. This seemed like a good idea, for non-swimming parents in particular it provided an 'introductory course' alongside their children. The others took to the water like ducklings, and several could float and dog-paddle alone within a few weeks – but not Louise. She didn't like her face being splashed, and although happy in her mother's arms didn't want to let go and move her arms or legs independently. In the end the instructress said, 'She's just not ready, and it's silly to pay for lessons at this point. She's one of the lazy ones who won't be ready to learn until she's 2, so bring her back then.'

The mother said, 'The instructress was lovely with the children, but the idea of "lazy" children not learning to swim until they were 2 shocked me to the core.'

She went on to say that she suddenly saw she had been trying to hurry Louise – who was indeed a lazy baby in the sense of being happy and contented – in all sorts of other ways, too. Then she added, 'If you can't take your time when you're still in your first two years, when can you?'

So she had slowed down, and was content to enjoy being in the water together, just for the pleasure it gave both of them. And already Louise was feeling free to let-go and enjoy being in water, and she will indeed take her back at 2 if Louise is ready to enjoy the next stage.

Most of us can remember seeing screaming children being carried into the sea by determined parents, or children standing knee-deep being splashed with icy water, and being told, 'Come on, it's lovely!' We can't 'make' children enjoy the water, and until they do enjoy the water they are not ready to learn to swim. If their confidence has already been shaken, then it is important to allow sufficient time (the child's idea of 'sufficient', not ours) and happy experiences for the fear to be resolved and genuine pleasure to take its place.

Also bear in mind that sometimes those with whom we are emotionally involved don't make the best teachers. Parents aren't always the best people to teach their children to swim. But bear in mind, too, that with swimming as with typing or playing the piano, the right technique early on makes all the difference to later performance.

Do make full use of your nearest swimming baths, and the excellent teachers they employ. Learning to swim is part of our survival kit, and can give so much pleasure as well as an ideal form of exercise right up to old age.

THE IMPORTANCE OF THE SENSE OF SMELL

I have just had an eye-opening reminder of how beautifully nature paves the way for children to grow up to be confident and secure, if only we will make time for it to happen. I was staying with a family who have a 25-month-old son we'll call James, and was struck with his mother's unhurried approach to each day. As she put it, 'My job was one long rush, and after living with computers I find James infinitely more rewarding. I could watch him all day.'

On this particular morning James had, as usual, been downstairs to have breakfast in his pyjamas and slippers, had fetched his father's lunch sandwiches from the fridge, pulled his coat from the back hall to the front door, and pointed to the car keys on a hook above the door. After a last kiss and a wave through the window James then made his way upstairs for the next part of the daily ritual – washing, then dressing in his warm bedroom. The first thing James registered was that his blanket as well as his sheets had been stripped off his bed, and that the clean blanket was hanging over the rails of his cot. He pulled it on to the floor, opened it as best he could, sat down and with careful deliberation began to bite and suck the ribbon binding at spaced intervals along the top and bottom edges. There was no 'naughtiness' in this, it was quietly purposeful, and we both sat and watched. Every now and then James would sit back and survey the mass, then lean over to bury his face in it, then pick up an untouched piece of binding and start to suck and chew again. Eventually his clean blanket began to feel and smell comfortably familiar, and the next part of the 'clean blanket day' ritual began. His mother explained later that usually all his bedtime friends were then bundled into the blanket, smothered, pulled out, and then bundled up again until they had added their own smell to the unwelcome cleanliness. On this occasion, however, a new ritual was added – Cat was offered a few bites along the binding, and then Duck had several inches stretched and pulled through his beak.

All this time James was oblivious of us. This was no playing to the gallery, or putting-off getting dressed. There was serious work to be done, and it took all his concentration and considerable effort. Only when everything felt and smelled right again did this endearing child get to his feet, heave the blanket over to his cot, and try to push it over the dropped side together with all his animals. He then co-operated happily in every stage of his dressing.

His mother said it had taken her some time to understand what was happening, but because he is such a happy, easy child she had assumed that there was a clue there somewhere if only she could find it. James didn't have a special piece of cuddly blanket or cloth, he had always sucked the ribbon binding of whatever blanket was on the bed. It was only slowly that she began to register that he took longer to settle on those nights when he had a clean blanket; at first she thought the extra sucking indicated hunger. But having understood she then noticed that he began to register the clean blanket in the morning, and concluded that it would be easier for everyone if the familiarization process took place then rather than at night.

This was borne out one morning when she was in a hurry, and had to whisk James away from his self-imposed task before it was finished to his satisfaction. He showed genuine distress, and that night the frantic sucking began again. Now she sees to it that the blanket is only changed on a morning when she can give him as much time as he needs.

Children have an animal-sharp sense of smell. One anxious little girl used to take her mother's nightie to bed if she was left with a baby-sitter, saying 'I feel safe when I can smell you.'

James was at the stage when his own reassuring scent (nothing to do with wet nappies) gave him just that much more confidence than an impersonal blanket.

No wonder James is more fascinating than a mechanical computer – he is a real live one. Already his own scent is enough to trigger the feeling, 'It's all right . . . I am in familiar territory and feel safe and comfortable with myself.'

PLAYING WITH DOUGH

Every parent knows those days when children are bored and restless and complain that 'there's nothing to do'. We make a dozen helpful suggestions, all of which are rejected, and finally we say, 'You've got a cupboard full of toys, and there are plenty of children who haven't got any, and if you can't find anything to do that's just too bad!' To which they reply, 'There's nothing worth playing with.'

If the toy cupboard only contains plastic bits and pieces that stack, roll, screw, interlock or press together, in identical red, blue, yellow and green, they've got a point. All these things have a well-loved place in the scheme of things, but there comes a time when the look, feel and colour of plastic is unsatisfying. Children need to get to grips with something quite literally, and few substances are more satisfying to the hands and emotions than dough.

Tip a large bag of *self-raising* flour into a bowl. Make a well in the centre, slowly pour in about a pint of cold water, and mix it with your hands (resist the use of the food mixer) for about ten minutes. Add about another ¼ pint and continue to work it until the lump is soft enough to squeeze without making your hands tired; this will take about ten minutes more, but it's worth it.

Leave it for a few minutes, and when you go back it will probably feel too stiff for comfortable handling. Wet your hands and work the dough until the water is absorbed, repeat until the lump is so slack, smooth and soft that you can pull and stretch it into a rope, and if you hold it up it will slowly droop down under its own weight. At this point play with it yourself for a while until you begin to sense what your child will discover. The dough will become warm and satin-smooth as you nip, squeeze, pummel and punch. If you poke deep finger holes, you can watch them fill up again as the self-raising agent does its work (plain flour will give a quite different type of dough, and the holes will remain holes).

Children may enjoy it plonked down on a table or tray just as it is, but some prefer to sit down and have it on their laps – dough is very clean, and an apron or one of dad's old shirts worn back to front is protection enough.

Just let the handling go on as long as it is satisfying, and when interest wanes put the dough in a plastic bag, wrap it so that no air is left inside, and put it in the fridge. It will keep for about a week before it begins to smell sour (the addition of a large tablespoonful of salt would enable it to be kept longer, but the dough won't handle in the same satisfying way, and the salt is painful for cuts or tender skin).

Children who are angry find it particularly satisfying to pinch, punch and bash, and the dough just absorbs it all without retaliation. A large wooden spoon offers more scope still, and if you hear a gleeful 'I'm smacking the baby!' don't be alarmed. This is nature's way of releasing deep feelings through play, where no harm will be done. It is natural to resent the baby sometimes and no child should be made to feel guilty about that, or guilty about smacking his substitute baby. Just be glad that a safe outlet has been found, and say something like, 'That makes a lovely sound, doesn't it?' or 'Does that feel very good?' You will innocently be referring to the dough and the spoon, and the pinching, smacking hands, but the unspoken communication between you is that you understand each other without direct reference to the baby at all.

Other variations are to colour the dough with vegetable dyes, or powder paint, or to offer large butter beans or buttons to be 'buried' only to rise to the surface like magic. But do give children time to go through all the simple, natural stages of discovery and exploration before offering any variations on the theme.

If the dough becomes too dry or stiff, let your child be the one to dip hands in water to work it back to the right consistency; and if it becomes too sticky, sprinkle on more flour. It is this 'doing' and 'feeling' that is at the very heart of play.

This form of play isn't to be confused with 'cooking', which is something else in its own right. 'Cooking' is associated with pastry, rolling pins, bun tins, and a product that can then be cooked and eaten; this is something to be connected with you, and homemaking, and is equally valuable in this context.

Playing with dough is different; the large mass of 'stuff' is just there to explore, and to act as a compliant lump to receive whatever the child chooses to inflict upon it, be it angry feelings or harmonious handling.

If you use an electric mixer to prepare the dough it will be quicker, but you miss the heart of the experience of which countless parents have said, 'I started to make it for *them*, but I became hooked on it. It's therapeutic, isn't it?'

Only as we begin to learn through our own experience how children 'feel' when they play will we find the time, energy and willingness to make the less familiar, and messy, types of play possible.

BEING SUNG TO

There are some people who are tone deaf and can't sing even the simplest scale or song in tune. If you are one of these for goodness' sake don't let it stop you singing to your children. A child who doesn't know the in-tune version of 'Baa Baa

Black Sheep' won't be in the least put out by a tuneless performance. As long as you enjoy yourself what will register with delight is that you are doing something different with your voice. It isn't talking, or whispering, or shouting, it is another way of using your voice altogether.

Learning is a magic circle. If you sing (with enjoyment) your child will want to share that pleasure with you, and will try to copy. Even if you sang like a nightingale the chances are that your child would begin by singing all on one note, either high or low, or in a series of uncontrollable highs and lows which are a most gratifying surprise, leading to the desire to go on practising this new discovery. Singing comes first, singing in tune is usually much later.

You can't start singing to children too early, and if you don't know any nursery rhymes then sing something you do know and enjoy – for your enjoyment will be conveyed, and the rhythm will be 'felt'. We are all responsive to rhythm, and if you think about it you will know that whether you are knitting, slicing beans, hammering nails, or cleaning windows you slowly slip into the rhythm of the job. And when you have the rhythm of that particular job your hands seem to move by themselves and you are at one with yourself and the job. So it is with rocking babies, or walking or dancing hand in hand with children, the rhythm establishes itself and brings harmony and pleasure.

In finger rhymes and jingles you can share togetherness and fun, and for those who 'don't sing', or 'can't sing' they are a good beginning. Many is the parent and grandparent who has been reminded of the pleasures of singing again by embarking on 'Round and round the garden, like a teddy bear . . .' with a much-loved baby.

Nursery rhymes have age old value, they are clear and simple in tune and rhythm, and an incidental bonus lies in the greatly increased vocabulary a child will acquire without either of you even realizing it. Don't worry about explaining the words (unless you are asked), just let them sink in through happy repetition.

Grandparents, and even great-grandparents, can all sing songs of their youth. 'It's a long, long, way to Tipperary' is still satisfying to sing, so are many of the old music hall songs, and the two most sung words of any Beatles' song must surely be, 'Yellow-sub-marine-yellow-sub-marine'!

Some people left school with the feeling that they couldn't

'do' music or art, and have never tried again. But our children give us a chance to go back to the beginning and find our lost confidence. Sing about the house, anything and everything, and if your unused voice cracks a bit at first it doesn't matter – just have a go!

SHARING PICTURE BOOKS

Reading is the ability to translate symbols into meaning, and the first printed symbols children learn to 'read' are pictures – words come much later. So start by looking at picture books together.

At first the pleasure and satisfaction come from being cuddled up on a warm lap, having your undivided attention, and basking in the tone of voice that says all is well between you.

Children enjoy this stage long before they begin to recognize the pictures, and they recognize the pictures long before they even begin to understand them. Quite early on they develop a memory for colour, shape and the order of pages, and can say the word that matches the picture – 'Lion . . . tiger . . . elephant . . .' But if an elephant paraded down the street it is by no means certain that they would point and say, 'Oh look, an elephant!'

Small pictures bear so little relation to the real life-size object, or to objects children have actually met, that they are often confused. One young television circus addict came in from the garden holding a large slug on her hand, saying 'Look, I've found a sea lion!'

But eventually connections are made, and the picture of a kettle is recognized whether it is in a story book or a magazine advertisement, even though it may be different in size, colour and design from the kettle in your kitchen.

The next stage is learning to look at pictures in sequence, so that one leads on to the next and a story evolves. The pictures may be accompanied by simple sentences, but your child won't know you are 'reading' because your voice will be 'talking'. Only later do children begin to understand that you seem to have the magic ability to look at black squiggles on a page, and turn them into a story.

At this stage children often delight in 'reading' a familiar book aloud to themselves with perfect accuracy, until your hopes are dashed by discovering that if two pages are turned together by mistake your child continues to recite regardless! Or they may open a book, upside down as often as not, and 'read' a made-up story.

All children need the *opportunity* to share the slow enjoyment of these early stages with you, but do bear in mind that some children have neither the time nor the inclination to be cuddled or read to. Don't worry, just let them come to it in their own good time.

FINGER GAMES AND RHYMES

There was a time when toys were only given to children at Christmas and on their birthdays, for the very simple reason that there was no money with which to buy them. It took weeks or even months to save up for those two presents.

Now toys abound, and for many children they are available all the year round. Sometimes they are carefully chosen to meet new stages of growth and development, sometimes they are loving gestures from friends and relations, and sometimes they are bribes or conscience salvers.

But if we aren't watchful toys will take the place of games played together, especially those games that didn't depend on toys at all.

Manufacturers draw your attention to the fact that your child will miss out if you don't buy their latest products, but none of them will buy advertising time or space to tell you that your child will miss out much more if you don't draw on your own store of memories to give them nursery rhymes and finger games.

'Round and round the garden, like a teddy bear. . .' still seems to be alive and well. 'Incy wincy spider' and 'Two little dicky birds sitting on a wall' don't seem to be equally well known any longer, and if it wasn't for playgroups and nurseries the whole wonderful range of finger games might be lost to children for ever.

The fact that children love them (given the chance) is self-evident. Once learned they are asked for again and again, and we only have to watch their faces to see the enjoyment they give. We also only have to watch their hands to realize the difficulty they have in learning to move their fingers and thumbs individually.

These early rhyming games and songs were rooted in real needs, they weren't just to keep children good, quiet and amused.

If you watch a baby's hands you will see that they are exquisite, with perfect little nails and a grip of primitive strength. Then they grow up and try to handle toys and spoons and mugs, with varying degrees of success. If they can use the whole of their hand in an encompassing grip, all is more or less well, even though the angle and speed of tipping a mug may be disastrous at first. The difficulty begins when they want to use their fingers for picking up small objects, or putting things into or on to other things, then they become fascinated or frustrated by what their fingers will and won't do.

Look at every child's hands you see during the coming week, and you will become aware of so much that you overlooked before. To begin with, their hands vary every bit as much as their feet in size and proportion. There are small claw-like hands, with very thin mobile fingers; there are soft fleshy hands with pudgy little fingers that can't seem to get the feel of things at all, unless the objects are large; there are fingers with sensitive tips which run over surfaces almost as though they are reading braille, and others which hate the feel of anything sticky, rough or messy; there are wonderfully strong hands which build, twist, thread and carry with efficient certainty; there are anxious fingers which push, pat and dab with little success, and many children find that even when the guiding brain and eye tell them what to do, their fingers don't seem to obey.

A lot of the difference is to do with size and shape; some relates to practice, or lack of it, in handling and manipulating objects and materials; and some is to do with courage and confidence, or the early feeling of defeat which comes from endless corrections and admonishments.

The value of finger games lies in the fact that the two of you are enjoying yourselves and each other, and that the children are first watching your fingers while trying to copy with their own, and then, when the rhyme and its movements have been memorized, they will actually watch their own fingers. This is the point at which real effort and learning begins, for they begin consciously to 'will' the individual fingers to move as they want them to, and slowly they will begin to obey. Obedient fingers and thumbs make so many later tasks, like learning to write numbers and letters, plait hair, pump up a bicycle tyre, easier and more rewarding. But most of all they are for pleasure.

DRAWING AND PAINTING

Although children learn at varying speeds and different ages, the stages of growth and development they go through are remarkably consistent. Whatever their colour or country of origin babies learn to kick, to move by crawling, shuffling or rolling; to pull themselves up on their feet, and to walk. They cut their teeth in much the same order and at roughly the same age. They learn to make sounds, then copy them, then interpret them, and eventually learn to speak within a year or two of each other.

All this parents know, but it is much less widely known that children everywhere also go through a natural series of stages in learning to draw and paint – or they could and would if we made it possible. And it is important that we do, both for their sake and ours, because children who go through all the various stages of development at the appropriate time are happier and easier to live with. Also, the practising of each new skill makes a general contribution to their maturity.

It is important, right at the beginning, to be clear about one thing – in the early stages children's drawings and paintings have absolutely nothing whatever to do with drawing an object, let alone 'doing a picture'. Drawing and painting are discoveries about marks on paper, colours and combinations of marks and colours; at first they are random, and then later choice and decision become possible, or imagination takes over. Then the whole process begins to flow and feelings can often be expressed on paper as well as in other ways. One child arrived at playgroup furious with his mother, made a beeline for the easel and covered a sheet with black paint, then he gave it a second coat before he sighed with satisfaction and played perfectly happily. When his mother came to collect him he offered her his black sheet saying, 'Do you know what this is? It's a growl.'

In painting children can lose themselves, and be at one with their thoughts and feelings. It is quiet, peaceful, creative, and sometimes therapeutic – part of nature's plan to enable children to express themselves in their own way without having to struggle to find words. Sometimes even to say the things they couldn't bring themselves to put into words; many a child will draw a large dominant figure and then grind it into a hole in the paper!

It can also be an expression of joy. Every playgroup knows the sheets of paper covered with beautiful patterns of colours swirled, dabbed, squiggled and splodged on with gay abandon or thoughtful care.

It's never too young to begin – 2 or 3 years old is fine. Use large sheets of paper pinned to a board propped up against a wall, a non-spill paint pot with a large hog's hair brush, and some powder paint mixed to a rich consistency that neither drags nor drips. At first the magic is dipping the brush in the paint and reaching out to splodge it on the paper, then repeating this again and again. Next comes lines, dots, dashes, patches and finally a sheet of colour with no paper showing. Day after day children will return to recapture the satisfaction, while you have the peace and pleasure of watching.

Once the idea has caught on a homemade or bought easel really is a good investment, together with more paint pots (with a brush in each) and bright colours – red, blue, yellow and black to begin with. The discovery will eventually be made that when some colours touch on the paper and run into each other they make a new colour.

An endless supply of paper will be needed: non-shiny wallpaper, computer paper, double thicknesses of newspaper. Also try the satisfaction of thick absorbent sugar paper bought from an art shop or the local branch of the Pre-school Playgroups Association. The initial outlay in money and organization is a sound investment, for each new stage of development will absorb the child deeply. And you will have the satisfaction of knowing that you are working with nature as you make it possible for children to develop creative imagination, communication and emotional health, and to lay the foundation of later writing skills through their painting.

STORIES BEGINNING 'ONCE, WHEN I WAS A LITTLE GIRL (OR BOY) . . .'

I remember the delight with which we used to listen to my mother and father telling us about the things they did when they were children.

A particular favourite was the story about my father and his younger brother misbehaving and being chased by their irate mother, brandishing her largest wooden spoon. They ran down through the orchard to the pond, clambered into an old barrel, and pushed off into the middle, where they stayed. What they had done to deserve such wrath, and how they got out, and what happened next was always a mystery. But that didn't matter, for one of the pleasures was watching Father's face twinkle-up in the telling, and hearing the chuckle in his usually rather gruff voice.

The other aspect that never ceased to intrigue was the blurring of images. On the one hand there were two small boys in a barrel, with their mother running round the pond waving the spoon and shouting; on the other was the mind-boggling image of Father and the even bigger Uncle Stan squashed into a small barrel, while Grandma waddled round the pond in her black dress with two aprons and her black jet necklaces.

Mother used to recount how school began every morning with exercises accompanied by the chanting of multiplication tables. It was easy enough to imagine her from her early photographs, but what brought it alive was the fact that whenever we were doing homework and said 'What are seven nines?' she could always answer instantaneously.

Children need us to tell them as much as we can remember about our childhood, and our parents. It is comforting to know that we were naughty, clumsy, thoughtless and frightened as well as happy, proud, clever and good – in fact, that we were just like them. It also gives a sense of continuity. Behind parents are their parents, and they were all children once; and ahead lies a grown-up life when they may one day have children of their own.

These stories also help us to remember what it felt like to be a child, and often to see our parents with new insight and forgiveness. Sometimes we begin by blaming our parents, and end up blaming theirs instead.

SOLVING PRACTICAL PROBLEMS

School days have left many people with a fear of maths which hampers them in everyday life. I was with a friend recently, measuring a house for carpets and curtains, and converting the length and breadth of each room into square yards made her anxious to the point where her hand shook as she tried to work it out in her notebook. She counted on her fingers and murmured, '3 into 17 won't go . . . wait a minute . . . it's 5 feet and 2 over . . . no, 5 yards and 2 feet . . .' Then she put down her pencil and said, 'Silly, isn't it? I could do this perfectly well on my own, but having you beside me takes me right back to my school desk, with Miss Saunders standing over me, waiting to pounce.'

Many parents feel like this, and knowing that they can't 'do' maths they are particularly concerned that their children shall have a head start before they go to school. To this end they count anything and everything in sight, and introduce problems into every activity, 'How many tarts have we got in the tin now? And how many more do we need to fill the tin? . . . There, all done . . . Now how many have we got?' The *idea* of wanting children to be happy and confident with numbers is fine, but not if it leads to a child being fed up and bored with cooking and our whole do-gooding approach to their lives.

One teacher told a story against herself: she counted stairs, washing on the line, peas in pods, cars going by the bus-stop and just about everything else in sight. Then one day she put a plate of beans on toast, topped by an egg, in front of her 4-year-old daughter, who sighed deeply and said, 'Mummy, I can see there's one egg, but do I *have* to count all the beans? Couldn't I just eat them?'

Mathematics isn't just numbers and sums, it is the abstract science of space and number, and the solving of problems and, just as important, it relates to everyday living, so *that* is where children need their pre-school experience.

I recently watched a 2-year-old getting his animals out of his cot to take downstairs, and was amazed how much he knew about distance and weight, things which we take for granted, but wouldn't if we saw them through the eyes of a child. He put one hand casually through the bars for a small bear, then a ladybird. He knew just by looking that the cat was out of reach, so he stood on tiptoe, clutched a bar with one hand, pressed his face and body as close to the cot as he could, and thrust the other arm through to its furthest extent; his fingers just touched the cat, and a few scratching movements inched it near enough to grab and pull through. He also knew by looking that Big Arthur was out of reach completely, so he pulled the cot away from the wall, went behind, and thrust both arms through to cope with the extra weight. He had even learned how to swing his arms up quickly to bring the unwieldy Big Arthur flying over the top rail of the cot with a deft flick of the wrists. I wondered how long it had taken him to learn when to let go of Arthur's beak, and how to manage the flick that left his precious bird outside the cot instead of back where it started!

I also watched, together with a maths lecturer, a film showing a 3-year-old trying to climb through a triangular climbing frame 'window' with a bar across. He put his hands on the bar and tried to get his leg over it, but the space was too small for the assortment of hands, knee, foot and head that he tried so hard to manipulate. Again and again he tried, and failed, first with one knee and then the other, but after heroic courage and effort he finally gave up and retreated the way he had come. And the mathematician said, 'This happens so often, in life as well as maths. Because he had decided to solve the problem in the way he first tackled it, his mind was closed to any alternative possibilities. In this case all he had to do was to crawl *under* the bar, where the space was wider, instead of trying to climb over it where the space narrowed towards the apex of the triangle.'

Count with children when it is natural, such as going up and down stairs when it can enliven a repetitive process. Give real life opportunities for them to become manually and visually experienced in relating sizes to spaces, like finding the right saucepan to hold the brussels sprouts.

Above all, help yourself, as well as your children of all ages, by tackling every problem with the confidence which says, 'Never mind if this doesn't work – we'll find another way.'

BEING READ TO

Not all children love being read to, and there is nothing to be gained by forcing the issue. And of those who do love it, no two are the same. Only you know your children, and only they know what they want and need at any particular time.

Sometimes children need stories that are simple and gentle to the point (you may think) of being boring, but they won't ask for the endless repetition of something that is boring to them.

At other times they enjoy stories where their hopes are raised and dashed by turn. Perhaps the central character has lost something precious and looks here . . . but no . . . there . . . but no . . . and somewhere else . . . but no . . . then, hey presto, there it was all the time.

Some children enjoy being positively frightened before the happy ending, whilst others shut the book with a bang saying, 'We don't want that one, do we?', to which the answer is 'No, not today.' At a later stage they may be like a 3-year-old who used to interrupt to say, 'In a minute will he go home and have an eggy for his tea, all warm and safe?' If the answer was Yes, then the story could continue.

Some of children's fears are so real that they can only live through them in story form if the characters are animals rather than themselves. The story of a baby bird looking for its mother is much less frightening than one about a child being lost.

Children have a lively sense of the absurd and usually love stories of people or animals who do silly things, or have mishaps, which appeal to their sense of fun. But part of the enjoyment lies in the satisfaction of being clever enough to recognize the errors of those who are less wise and knowledgeable than they are.

You may find that under-fives are less than enthusiastic about traditional fairy stories. They still find it so difficult to distinguish between reality and imagination, and the sort of fantasy in which things happen that break all the facts of life that they are just beginning to understand tends to confuse, bore or frighten them. Enjoyment of fairy stories usually comes several years later.

Many children become addicted to one particular story, which you read until you could scream – and woe betide you if you aren't word perfect! But go along with it while it obviously meets some inner need.

Do make full use of your local children's library, and allow *plenty* of time for your child to settle and browse through the big open boxes of books specially arranged for them, before choosing the books to take home. But remember that children can become suddenly exhausted through concentration and the wide choice available. Select one book yourself, so that if those your child finally hands to the librarian give less pleasure than anticipated, there will be one that is almost sure to be a success.

WHERE REALITY, IMITATION AND FANTASY MEET IN PLAY

How imaginative are you? Some people can look at a small sample of wallpaper or material and imagine exactly how it will look on the wall or made up into a dress. Others can't make the imaginative leap at all. And some visualize it so inaccurately that they are bitterly disappointed when confronted by reality.

Imagination is an elusive quality, partly coloured by our emotions, but fundamentally it is the ability to transform the appearance or character or disposition of things in our mind's eye. It is a precious and enriching gift, and one that is rapidly becoming extinct in our materialistic way of life; do guard it in your children.

Just like us, there are sensitive imaginative children; those who are solidly practical and down-to-earth; those whose imagination spills over into fantasy, and carries them into a world of their own as they play; and those whose anxiety colours their lives with fearful imaginings. They, too, are wishful thinkers, and will exaggerate, or make their tale good – and if we know we do all these things from time to time we will understand and be kind.

Children have an enchanting ability to transform objects in their imagination as they play. Do watch out for it, and when you see it leave well alone; don't be tempted to supply the 'proper' thing.

I know a 2½-year-old who loved watching his mother iron. He used to pat and smell the smooth warm hankies as they were added to the pile, and never tired of watching the iron as it glided up and down the board. One day he was playing with a longish narrow block of wood which contained peg-men, when he stopped dead with a 'thinks!' look on his face. Then he removed the little men, grasped the block firmly in the middle, and began to 'iron' the carpet . . . then the chair seats . . . then the curtains against the wall . . . then the jumper on his tummy. He ironed his way round the house day after day with deep concentration and satisfaction. Then he grew tired of it. Then he found a pyjama cord in the mending bag, seized upon it with great purpose, found his pretend-iron, and stuffed one end of the cord into the end hole – he then had an iron with a flex, and started ironing all over again, till that, too, grew stale. Then one day he looked at the drying-up cloth hanging from its wall suction cup – and went off to find his iron and the pyjama cord. Out came the tea towel (on to the floor, naturally, because his mind was racing ahead), into its place went one end of the pyjama cord – and he had an electric iron, complete with flex and power point. But this tied him to one spot, so the only thing to iron was the tea towel on the floor – which he did, up and down, and across, and folded again and again exactly as his mother had folded the hankies.

He would have been deprived of all these hours of imaginative play, based on the real experience of ironing, had his mother said, 'Christopher! put that pyjama cord back – how can I mend Daddy's pyjamas if you lose it?' or 'No! Put the tea towel back in its holder where it belongs.'

So often our training and teaching cuts across nature's training and teaching. Sometimes we do have to intervene – of course we do. But quite often if we really looked at what our children were doing, and understood why, we would marvel at their intelligence and let well alone.

Christopher's latest play has been sparked off by his father's work on the car during a week's holiday at home. He now lifts up the centre cushion on the settee and thrusts it up against the back, then having 'lifted the bonnet' he leans over and digs his fingers into the various bits of the imaginary engine. This is enough for the time being, but my guess is he will soon be inventing dipsticks, cans of oil, funnels, spanners and everything else he can remember.

Much of real play is about noticing, remembering, reproducing the objects and practising and skills needed in adult life. In one way it is a preparation for adult life, and yet at the child's level it is pure play at its most inventive and creative – the very stuff of childhood.

GOING ON HOLIDAY

Some children can have things sprung on them at a moment's notice, and take it in their stride quite happily. Others are bewildered and miserable if they are not well prepared in advance for the slightest change in routine, let alone a holiday.

Children need to be included in holiday preparations, not just for their understanding but for the pleasure and learning that are part of the planning. Whether it is camping, a stay with relatives, a package holiday abroad, a farmhouse or seaside holiday, or day outings from home it is helpful if the visible signs of preparation begin to build up one or two weeks in advance. As you gather together clothes, maps, food, toilet and first aid items, or whatever your particular holiday calls for, so the children can gather together what they want to take.

I can remember the washing and ironing of our dolls' clothes that went on, and the assembling of toys and games, and the relief of being told that there would only be room for one small case, for the whole thing had become a worry. I can also remember one occasion when room was found for all that I wanted to take, and what a burden it was on holiday, for I didn't want any of it. But it taught me a lot.

Only you know your children. Find a small case or basket for their personal belongings, and let the size of it be related to *them* as much as to the available space. But try not to pin them down too tightly for learning comes through mistakes as well as success.

Some children have only a hazy notion of days and 'We go on holiday next Saturday' doesn't have any real meaning. Anxious children find it easier to understand 'We go when we have had four more sleeps.'

Let them in on all the other jobs that have to be done, too. Newspapers and milk to be cancelled, and arrangements made for animals and house plants. If we are aware that we are helping children to learn how holidays are planned, it helps us to become more methodical ourselves.

But why, oh why, do some of us feel that curtains have to be washed, drains cleaned and fridges defrosted when we know perfectly well that they wouldn't be done if we stayed at home? I still feel this urge – though I'm getting better. It is good to come home refreshed to a house looking as good as we feel; but it is a pity to waste the first three days of a holiday by being too tired to enjoy them.

CARING FOR A PET PLANT

Some children have a great affinity for plants at a very early age. I knew a 2-year-old who so loved and identified with the golden nasturtiums he planted himself outside the back door that each morning he would save the last drops of his milk, and the last piece of toast, to go and give them their breakfast. They grew and flourished, and with a little help he learned to pick the flowers without pulling up the root, and to arrange them in a small vase and put them by his bed. He had a real relationship with those nasturtiums, and as they had water when they were extra thirsty, and the birds ate the toast crumbs when no one was around, it would have been insensitive and unnecessary to 'teach' him about plant foods at that point. What mattered was that he wanted to look after them in his way, and in return they gave him flowers in profusion.

A 7-year-old had a busy-lizzie on his bedroom window-sill. The satisfactory thing about these plants is that they wilt quickly and visibly when they are short of water, revive just as quickly if their obvious need is met, and they are very tolerant of over-watering. They also grow quickly, and have a profusion of flowers in lovely bright oranges, pinks or reds. This particular child kept a score of the number of flowers, and I was invited to admire it on the day that it had 72 perfect cerise blooms all out together.

I remember being ill when I was a child and a Mrs Cockerill arriving with a present for me. No words can describe how I felt when she handed me what looked like a tiny fir tree hung with purple bells, growing in the smallest flowerpot, and standing in its own miniature china dish (which I still have). The plant stayed on the window-sill long after it had died, and I was grateful that mother made no comment. It was *my* heather, and it was left to me to deal with in my own way. Eventually I planted it in the garden, knowing it couldn't come to life again, but feeling it was somehow more appropriate than the dustbin or the compost heap.

Pot plants can make delightful gifts for either boys or girls, but they need to be small. Bigness suggests self-sufficiency, but small things tend to spark a protective instinct. They also need to be given together with a tiny plastic vase-filling watering-can, one that is a joy in its own right and will encourage regular watering.

There are some plants to avoid. Beware of azaleas, they only have to be short of water for a few hours for the flowers to droop, never to revive. On the other hand a child who is methodical and enjoys ritual may enjoy instituting a system whereby the watering-can is filled each night after teeth cleaning, carried into the bedroom and put beside the plant, and then used each morning to give it a good drink of water at room temperature. You must know your child.

Cyclamen can be tricky, too, unless the child's bedroom is evenly warm (not hot). The plant can be in full light, and the watering is done from the bottom and not the top.

One tomato plant in a large plastic flower-pot, together with written instructions and a small packet of tomato plant food, may well delight the right 7-year-old or older.

Or one pansy in its own big pot to stand outside, or an indoor Christmas cactus which is so accommodating about being more or less ignored after it has flowered and been put outside to rest.

Start slowly, one plant can be a pleasure, two or more a burden in the early days.

PLAY LUDO

The coming of television has denied a great many children the breadth and depth of learning that used to be acquired so happily when children and parents played card or board games together. As a refresher for those who have forgotten, let's just consider the many strands of learning woven into a simple game of ludo.

The age at which children are ready to play varies according to temperament and experience, it may be 4, or 6, or later. The basic necessities for the child are that he or she wants to play, is capable of concentrating, can count up to six, and knows which colours are red, blue, yellow and green. The basic necessities for you are that you have the time and temperament to be patient, and that you don't consciously or subconsciously need to win (if you do, for goodness' sake recognize the fact, ask yourself Why? and try to do something about it before you become the sort of parent and person who always has to win every argument, have the last word, and sees to it by hook or crook that everybody does what you want them to do).

If all these basic criteria are met, then take it very slowly. Allow time for the unpacking of the box, and the handling of the counters, dice and shaker; in fact, spend some time taking it in turns to shake out the dice and see and say what it 'says'. Then let the child choose his or her colour, and you take the one diagonally opposite. Allow time for the counters to be placed very precisely on the white circles in the home-base, for children new to anything often find comfort in the feeling of power that precision brings.

The younger the child the more important it is to have another practice period, not only of throwing the dice and saying what it says, but then *doing* what it says. To begin with the child will need to tap or push the counter into each square individually, counting aloud at each move, and probably needing to pause and recount with a pointing finger, to make sure that the counter has reached the right place.

As you watch you will begin to realize how much of our own learning we take for granted – one glance at that distinctive cross formation of dots and our brain flashes 'five', but children need to count the dots again and again until they can recognize it on sight. This is where your patience comes in. If you are intent on getting on with the game you will watch the jerky throw and call out 'five!'. But if it is the playing and learning together that is the focus of your attention, you will sit peacefully and quietly while the child takes the full time necessary to look, find the right counter, move along the counted spaces, check the move if necessary, and savour the satisfaction of mastery over the whole process that constitutes a 'turn'. Only then will you pick up the shaker for your own slow and careful turn.

If you dash off your turn in two or three seconds, and then go back to knitting your sock or doing the crossword puzzle, the message your child receives is, 'I'm slow and clumsy and boring.' There isn't any value in playing if the message isn't 'What a lovely time we're having, and how clear and orderly it all is, and how capable and satisfied I feel.' After many games children begin to recognize the formations on sight, and can even pick up a counter and move it accurately from one place to another by counting with their eyes; later still they will 'know' where almost any throw will take them without counting at all.

Then comes the tricky bit of playing by the rules, learning to wait for the starting six without losing heart; learning to send or be sent home without excessive boasting or aggression, and yet learning to face up to, and come through, all these emotions for that is part of learning to live (it helps if the adult keeps his or her own emotions even, remembering that it is by our example that children learn most of all).

If children can master and enjoy ludo then you will know that they have also grasped the fundamentals of mathematics, which is the understanding of number and space, and the solving of problems.

AN OUTWARD EXPRESSION OF INNER ANXIETY, HOLDING ON TO FAECES

Some children go through a stage of not only refusing to use a potty, or the loo, but of seeming deliberately to prevent a bowel movement. As one mother described it, 'He'll be playing perfectly happily, and suddenly he'll go red in the face, grow very tense and hold-on. I say, "Do you want to go to the toilet?" and he shakes his head. If I try to take him he resists with all he's got.'

Other children refuse to let-go in the proper place, but will then relieve themselves in their pants or in a quiet corner behind a chair. And understandable enough parents feel upset, angry, guilty, ashamed, baffled, or a mixture of these emotions.

As always, there are several equally understandable reasons for all this. A child may be constipated, either occasionally or habitually, until a connection becomes established which indicates 'This is going to hurt, so I'll try not to let it happen.'

Even though you suspect constipation as the cause, do go to the doctor rather than administer a laxative; the 'explosive' type can be quite frightening, and some of us may remember the fear that all our blood and bones might come out in the rush as well as everything else. The doctor will know which of the many different types will be best to prescribe under the circumstances. And it may be that alterations to the diet are called for, for some children have such a highly efficient digestive system that not enough roughage is left for the bowel to act on easily.

Other causes are emotional rather than physical, but this doesn't mean that they are 'naughty', or 'trying it on'. Always we have to remember that children's feelings are even stronger than ours, and that since they haven't yet developed our ability to define and communicate our thoughts and feelings in words, the only way they can communicate is at the subconscious level of action.

A 3-year-old once had her secure world shaken three times in quick succession. If she had been old enough, and experienced enough to speak from real firsthand knowledge, she might have described her life before the shocks like this, 'I've got Mummy and Daddy, and we all live together in our warm safe cottage. And Auntie and Uncle live in the same village. We're going to have a new baby, so we are going to move to a lovely big house with a garden in the next village.' But then, out of the blue, the aunt died the day before the move, her parents were distraught as well as distracted, and at the end of that traumatic 24 hours the child was forced to change that description so that it went, 'Something terrible happened – I don't know what – Mummy cried, and Daddy wasn't the same. And men came and took everything away. And we were sent away to a big cold empty house.' That is how it must have *seemed*.

A few weeks later her mother went into hospital to have the baby, and had to stay longer than expected, so yet again someone precious disappeared suddenly. And when her mother returned the retention of faeces began. From the child's point of view the turmoil left her feeling that so much had been taken away from her she needed to hold on tight to all that remained, especially to the innermost 'self' that is the core of our personality. How can a 3-year-old understand that the 'self' isn't located in the bowels? We talk about a gut-feeling, and that is probably just what this child had: the gut-feeling that she'd better hold on – or else. Time and reassurance led to the child feeling safe enough to release her bowels in the security of her bed – more reassurance, and nappies, took the anxiety out of this stage, and eventually everything returned to normal.

The same symptoms appeared in a 2½-year-old, but for rather different reasons. In this case both parents were loving, conscientious and highly responsible people, but at every stage they expected a standard of behaviour that was beyond him. They wanted him to say 'Please' and 'Thank you,' to go to sleep straight away, to eat up all his food, to put his toys away, to be immediately obedient to their slightest suggestion, to be clean and quiet and good. And that word 'good' had nothing to do with morality, it really meant 'convenient to us'.

At first he tried and tried to please them, fearing to lose love if he didn't. And then he grew defiant, but they wouldn't let him get away with anything; always they won each battle. Until in the end he found the perfect way to hold his own – literally.

If his parents hadn't been so intent on 'controlling' him, they would have understood that this was his only way of saying, 'Stop crowding me. Take the pressure off. I can feel myself being ground-down, turned into a puppet instead of a person. I've tried to please. Now I'm fighting for survival. And I'm glad that a mess on your carpet drives you to distraction – for now you know what it feels like to be goaded beyond bearing.'

Once the general pressure was taken off, then gradually he became happy and relaxed, with a bowel movement to match.

If you are worried about the retention of faeces (with or without the smearing of them everywhere), do go and talk it over at the Child Guidance Clinic.

FEEDING THE BIRDS

If I had intended a completely different type of article I would have called this one 'Identification of Some Common British Birds' – but that's not what I think we should be about with children. Our passion for naming everything in sight, together with the correct colours and numbers, can switch-off children from curiosity, wonder, and a response to beauty, like a light going out.

I suggest we put away our pocket bird books and start from basics with our children; and that we promise ourselves we won't try to 'teach' them anything, we'll just watch and learn with them at their own level.

Whether or not children have previously taken any interest in birds a snap of cold weather can provide a new starting point. Children are loving, caring little people, with a fellow feeling for even smaller creatures out in the cold with nothing to eat or drink. The arousal of caring and interest leads to involvement, to taking action because the need is there and they want to respond to it. (This nurturing instinct, which is in both boys and girls, needs to be encouraged.) So start on a cold winter's day with, 'It's a hard frost this morning, we must feed the birds and give them some water.'

Contemplate *together* what to put the water in, but give enough clues to prevent the obvious response 'a mug', which would probably be followed by the typical adult put-down of 'No, because . . .'. Try 'they are only small, do you think they would like it in a saucer, or one of our flat baking tins, or a big soup plate?' Agree with whatever is chosen. Observation will tell you both whether birds like to stand on the ground and reach, or perch on a rim and dip, or stand on a wide rim and dip. But learn from the birds, not a book.

Similarly, let the children break the slices of bread into any sized pieces they choose; the birds will teach them whether they like it in crumbs, or pieces to peck at, or pieces to fly away with.

Then put both bread and water where you can watch to see what happens – too near the window and the birds may not come, too far away and you won't be able to see properly or keep an eye open for cats (a raised bird table can come a little later when interest is established).

Watching together is important, for efforts need to be crowned with success and shared. If the birds come, just share the child's satisfaction that when they fly away they aren't hungry or thirsty any more.

Once the habit is established, then you can both look and learn some more. Some birds swoop down on the food, some hop cautiously nearer, some even run. Sometimes the big birds scatter the smaller ones, and gobble everything in sight.

At this stage children are still emotionally involved with the birds, feeling sorry for the little ones, angry about the greedy ones, or proud of the fact that all the food has been eaten up, no matter by which birds.

It is this identification with the birds that leads on naturally to more learning. How are the little birds to be given a chance to eat their fair share? Buy or make a bird table with a roof over it which will prevent the bigger ones from getting at the food. At this stage the birds are likely to be so tame that a bird table could be erected quite close to a window, so that you can all see the birds individually in close-up, and such a table could be a lovely birthday or Christmas present for the right child.

Now the experiments and observations can really take off. A net of nuts hung out of cat-reach will attract the blue tits, so will half a coconut. *Experience* will teach that the obvious white-side-up leads to the coconut getting wet and going mouldy, so then the next one can be hung upside down. And miraculously there are birds that can cling on and peck upside down!

At this stage the birds and their habits will be familiar but you may want to know which bird is which, so now (and not before) is the time for an illustrated book in which you can identify well-known friends and learn their names.

HAVING TIME TO LOOK AND 'SEE'

There are several levels of seeing, as we all know if we stop to think about it. Take something simple, like getting in the washing. We may dash down the path, grab the clothes off the line, and dash in again, having 'seen' only where the path was, and the pegs as we stretched up for them. Or we may go down the path slowly, noticing the progress in the flower beds along the way, and even the clouds overhead as we tilt our heads back to reach for the pegs. Or we may notice all this, but also make judgements about the clothes – hankies too dry, put them on the still damp towels; drip dry shirts have blown smooth, don't crease them; bath mat still wet, the breeze will go on drying it for another hour even if it is nearly dark.

The garden, the sky, the washing on the line, are the same each time. What varies is the range and depth of our awareness, according to how much time we have, how much importance we attach to flowers and clouds in our lives, and how much we have learned (and care) about preparing clothes for ironing.

Take another example: the first day of a holiday in a strange place. The chances are we go exploring rather cautiously to get our bearings, stopping after the first turn or two to check-back mentally to our base. We may be content to enjoy the feeling of freedom, the freshness of it all, without registering anything in detail. Repetition on subsequent days fills in a few more details each time, mostly according to immediate needs – we need to buy food, to find a good beach for bathing and the bus stop. Later still as the consequence of daily experience we learn which beach is sheltered if the wind is off the land, which one loses the sun by early afternoon, which shop has the best bread, and where we can go for a meal that won't break the bank.

Our eyes have to learn to see detail as well as the broad sweep of things, and our brain has to learn to make connections so that we can interpret what we see.

So it is with the observation of our children. We suddenly register that they are suspiciously quiet, and hastily go in search of them. One broad-sweep glance interprets what they are doing as harmless, so back we go to preparing vegetables. Or we see in sharply defined detail that they are interfering with packets and tins in the store cupboard, and we tell them not to, because our brains have made sense of what they are doing to our nice tidy shelves, and rightly (from our point of view) we want to restore harmony to those well-ordered stores.

But once we have children we need to extend the art of our seeing yet again, to go beyond making-sense to us, so that it also includes seeing through the eyes of a child.

A child in the store cupboard may be 'seeing' sultanas for the first time. They have been half-seen and eaten before in buns and bread and butter puddings, but now they are being minutely inspected (and eaten, naturally). Before pouncing, do watch; when was the last time you actually looked at a sultana? Some of these small dried grapes still have their little stalks attached. They were once small seedless grapes grow-ing in bunches, like the small seedless grapes we can buy in the supermarkets in the summer. We know all this in theory, but familiarity has bred indifference so that we no longer 'see' with the curiosity, interest and wonder of a child learning about the world for the first time.

A child may break an egg, and with our first-sight we see the mess, and we register the waste of money – of course we do, it would be unintelligent if we didn't. But the child sees, hears, feels and senses that he has broken something and is distressed. If we can get beyond ourselves we shall be able to say, 'It's all right. I've done that lots of times. It was an accident. We can clear it up. Can you find some tissues, and the floor cloth?'

Education is based on seeing, and 'seeing'; and parents and grandparents are in a stronger position than anyone else to 'see' children; to understand what they are doing, thinking, watching, as they survey things for the first time – as we watched with awe as the first men rocketed to the moon.

BEING TOO BUSY FOR BOOKS

Our firstborn could have spent the first five years of his life very happily sitting on someone's lap being read to. Our quicksilver second child couldn't spare the time for a quick kiss in passing, let alone a cuddle; she was so busy living life to the full that she never had time to listen to a word anyone said, let alone a story.

As soon as our first child could read, he read avidly, and if his library books were finished he read the labels on jars and packets in the cupboard, and browsed among the pile of old newspapers.

Our second read her school books with efficient disinterest and hadn't the time for library books until she was 8 and, suddenly discovering fairy stories, read straight through the library's entire stock from every country. Then she didn't read for pleasure again until she discovered 'Perry Mason' in her teens.

No two children are alike, and parents should never feel pressured into reading books to unwilling children. Neither should they nag them (however pleasantly) to read for pleasure if, quite clearly, it isn't a pleasure.

One day I turned on the radio by chance and heard an

intelligent, cultured, educated woman saying that she had been brought up with books all her life. Whenever the family was going out anywhere her mother would always say, 'Have you got your cardigan and your book?', and if she was sitting in a chair doing nothing her mother would say, 'Where is your book?' She grew up loving books, reading avidly until well into her teens, 'And then', she said, 'I discovered life. And I've read hardly anything since.'

I found this comforting, because somehow we are all made to feel inadequate if we don't read much, and guilty if our children don't.

We are also made to feel that we should have a vast stock of reference books, or encyclopaedias (send every salesman packing), on hand, and lose no opportunity to help our children look things up. But I believe the introduction of such books too soon can rob children of a great deal of wonder, curiosity and private joy in the world that is still so new to them.

I remember my curiosity at seeing a shiny trail on the path one morning, and the satisfaction of finding a lovely shell at the end of a tracking expedition; it was curved and ridged, and patterned in greyish fawny browny colours. And as I looked a head poked out at one end, with little sticks waving about, and then the shell was lifted up and moved along, very slowly. I reached out to touch it, and both ends disappeared. It was thrilling. Sheer magic. And it would have been a disaster if anyone had intruded into that moment to name or explain the object of my interest, let alone diverted such close attention from my beautiful secret creature to a book. It would have been too soon.

I hope all this may have released some of you from the musts, oughts, pressures and guilty feelings that are so often associated with books. Once freed from guilt and resentment you might even come to enjoy reading one day.

'HURTING PAPER'

Recently I was sent a paper drawn up by parents, teachers, playgroup people and others, outlining ways in which children's transition from home to school could be eased. One of the recommendations was that young children needed soft toilet paper.

This simple, human suggestion struck a long-forgotten chord in my memory. I can remember how painful some papers were, they seemed to fold into sharp points and cutting edges. As one child said to her mother recently, 'Why does Grandma have hurting paper in her bathroom?'

My mind went back to so many memories I thought I had forgotten. We had Bronco paper at home, and I remember the pleasure I derived from the beautifully written purple signature on each sheet. And how useful it was for tracing, thin enough to see the picture underneath, and tough enough not to split under the pressure of the pencil applied to both sides. We also used to put it over coins, rub them all over with a soft pencil, and watch the imprint come through – then we cut them out, mounted them on cardboard, and had 'money' for our shopping games.

One grandmother had Izal, definitely hurting paper in those days – but the compensation was the two lines of Nursery Rhymes printed in green under the perforation of each sheet. I can remember sitting there one day and pulling the sheets down as I read each one. I didn't realize that there was a sequence which came to an end and then repeated itself, so I went on and on looking for a different one, until I suddenly became aware of the mass of shining paper coils round my feet.

The feeling of panic was terrible, I tried to rewind the roll, but it wouldn't go flat or straight, and eventually I had to leave the unwieldy mass jamming the holder on the wall and still straggling on to the floor. Since Mother knew how to put just about everything right I went to find her to tell her what had happened, and she explained to Grandma – who beamed, twinkled and laughed, 'Bless the child!' The relief and gratitude was a thousand times more effective than any scolding would have been.

But it was our paternal grandmother's home that held the best memories. There, you had to go out of the back door, and round past the coalhouse, water-butt, and shed where the broody hens sat under bushel baskets until their eggs were hatched. Then round the ivy-clad corner to the shrubbery, where the austere 'little house' lurked under syringa and nut bushes. The wide seat was scrubbed white wood, and sitting there was magical. The light filtered green and dim through the leaves outside the small high window, and there was no sound but the birds, or sometimes the wind or rain. It was a place of retreat, safety and silence.

There was no toilet paper here, only a large telephone directory slung on a loop of thick string from a six-inch nail. And sometimes, around Christmas, the orange or white squares of tissue paper in which oranges were wrapped – we were required to save them all, smooth them out, and put them in the little basket on the end of the wide seat. I much preferred the orange papers to the telephone directory.

And then the privacy was invaded by a large calendar from the Mothers Union which Grandma pinned up on the door. You could see all the months at a glance, and find your birthday, but you were also under the gentle scrutiny of Jesus – He stood there among the flowers, with a lamb in his arms, and just looked at you. This was very disconcerting under the circumstances. And when it was time for the orange papers there was a dilemma; to face Him and be embarrassed, or to turn my back and risk being not only rude but possibly blasphemous?

I met some of the group who had drawn up the recommendations, and said what a hopeful sign I thought it was when people began to draw on their own childhood memories in order to offer practical suggestions – like soft loo paper. Sadly, the answer was, 'Oh, that wasn't the reason. Parents were complaining that the children weren't cleaning themselves properly, and they were everlastingly having to wash knickers and pants.'

What a pity to do the right thing for the wrong reasons from the child's point of view.

VIDEO GAMES

This time last year I found myself standing beside a father and his daughter of about 8 years. They were looking at video games for her Christmas present, and had just reached the point of decision when she said, 'Can I have this one, too?', and he replied, 'No, £45 is enough at one go. You'll have to wait.' When they had gone I asked if many parents spent this amount of money on a young child's present, and was told, 'Yes. But he'll be back after Christmas – most of them will – because he's not intelligent enough to learn how to play.'

This left so many questions in my mind. Is a video game now the equivalent of a train set, bought ostensibly for the child but in reality to satisfy the parents' desire to play? And if parents find it difficult, couldn't they ask a neighbouring child who has mastered the art? If not, why not? And how does it come about that children pick up these games so much more readily than adults?

Recently I came across some studies of children and computer games undertaken in California, and although the number of families and schools was small the findings were interesting. In one study children aged 5–13 years were watched and questioned to try to analyse the appeal of a wide range of arcade games, simulations, adventure games and learning games. The children were unanimous in preferring video games to television, because they liked being personally involved, and what happens on the screen is not entirely determined by the computer, it is also influenced by the players' actions. Graphic games, for example, where two players control the action, were more popular than word games, for example a fill-in-the-blanks story about Goldilocks. And the most unpopular games had little or no animation. They liked the automatic score keeping, the sound effects, the element of chance, and the importance of speed, but the presence of a goal was the single most important factor in determining the popularity of games.

It seems there is evidence that violent video games breed violent behaviour, both *Space Invaders* and *Roadrunner* have been found to raise the level of aggressive play. But two-player aggressive video games, whether co-operative or competitive, *reduced* the level of aggression in children's play: It may be that the most harmful aspect of the violent video games is that they are solitary in nature. A two-person aggressive game seems to provide a releasing effect for aggression, whilst a solitary aggressive game (like *Space Invaders*) may stimulate further aggression.'

Video games need not have a violent content. The most popular game was a version of computer pin-ball. In other words, it is action, not violence itself, that attracts children. Incidentally, a game where balls knock down brick walls was more popular than those involving the bombing of sub-marines or shooting at Darth Vader's ship. Some children are actually alienated from arcade games because of their aggressive themes.

One very popular game was *Taxi*, where the goal is to drive a passenger through a city as quickly and efficiently as possible, overcoming obstacles on the way. In play tests children became increasingly co-operative as they became experienced with the game, and learned that co-operation paid off.

The message seems to be that the choice of games can have an important influence on children's behaviour, and contrary to what they may ask for, or think they want, it is action not violence that is the real attraction.

Fantasy games involved complex characters, with a mediaeval flavour, who went on adventures together and met a wide variety of circumstances and obstacles. The characters are composed of different combinations of six qualities – strength, IQ, luck, agility, vitality and piety – and children need to understand and construct multi-dimensional characters.

The eye and hand co-ordination skills of video games are valuable, not mindless. So, too, is children's growing aware-ness of different speeds, directions and characteristics of different parts of the screen. Action games may foster parallel processing skills and fast reactions, but discourage reflection. Some of the fantasy-adventure games allow unlimited time for reflection and planning, but these games are almost too responsive to the child's input. Too much control over the fantasy world of video games could bring about impatience and bafflement in the real world of human relationships.

Video games are rapidly becoming part of our culture, and we need to give considerable thought to the place they play in our children's lives.

PART FIVE

HEALTH AND SAFETY

PREVENTING PERMANENT DAMAGE TO CHILDREN'S FEET

Recently I spent a morning with a specialist in the care of children's feet, and I am delighted to be able to pass on what I learned. As always, some things I knew, some I didn't, and some advice left me thinking, 'How obvious, why didn't I think of that?'

The vast majority of feet are normal, and that means there is no obvious defect, and they are able to function for the purpose for which they are intended – to walk, run, climb, stand on tip-toe and generally move and support the body. But in appearance 'normal' feet vary even more widely than 'normal' hands. They may be short, long, wide, narrow, with high or low arches, long or short toes. They may even vary in the number of bones they have (even up to nine or ten supernumary bones) and still be regarded as normal feet.

Some children walk at 10 months, some at 2 years. The late walkers tend to be bigger children, who need more fully developed muscles to support them.

When babies are born they have only three real bones in their feet, all the rest are laid down as cartilage, with spaces between. As the feet grow these cartilages lengthen and harden until the foot is fully matured after eighteen years (though the growth in the last three years is usually minimal).

But in the early years the cartilage is so soft that it can be affected by the slightest pressure. This can have advantages as well as disadvantages; for example it has been found that two or three minutes of gentle stroking at each nappy change can effectively straighten some feet which are out of alignment, but do seek advice first and a demonstration from your clinic (where they are increasingly aware of this) because nature's idea of alignment and ours are not always the same.

It follows that if feet are this easy to manipulate great harm can be done at a very early age by any kind of restriction, so a few warnings are in order about the feet of baby-grows. The fact that these garments can be bought too large, and grown into, is invaluable, but babies' feet are particularly vulnerable as the baby grows and the garment shrinks in the wash. There was a photograph of a baby whose feet were already misshapen: the specialist commented that the baby-grow was too small, the parents demurred and demonstrated that the material was still not at full stretch. The specialist asked their permission to cut along the seam at the toes. Carefully pulling the material away from the feet he cut across, let go – and the legs of the garment sprang back to halfway between the ankle and the knee. Even the lightest pressure is enough to constrict and distort the fourteen minute cartilages that are in the toes alone.

Bearing this in mind pay particular attention to the size of the baby-grows, and leave children barefooted for as long as possible. When warmth is necessary then loose woolly boot-tees or leggings provide that without pressure, but bare-is-best is a good motto until children are ready to walk outside (providing floors are neither cold nor splintery).

When children begin to walk they are usually bow-legged, and by 2 years many children are slightly knock-kneed. Both these conditions usually right themselves, but if you are anxious go to the clinic. By 6 years most children's legs are 'normal' (but men tend to be slightly bow-legged, and women slightly knock-kneed).

The first seven years are the most vital, and by then all too many feet have suffered permanent damage. The only effective shoes for toddlers and children are lace-ups, bars and T-bars. Slip-ons are inadequate, pointed toes are obviously damaging, and sling-backs are worst of all because they neither hold the heel in position nor prevent the foot slipping forward to crush toes. All shoes should be fitted for width as well as length, and it is imperative that shoes are long enough.

Another point to remember is never fit new shoes over stretch socks. There was a tale to tell of a 7-year-old who had been referred for pain when she walked. Her shoes were put on her bare feet, and she walked without pain. Her shoes were removed and replaced by socks only, and she walked with pain. The socks were removed, the unstretched sock foot was compared with the length of her own foot, and it was $2\frac{1}{2}$ inches shorter. We underestimate the power of constriction of man-made fibres because they are so springy and light, but they are more than a match for the still-soft bones of a foot that have not yet joined up to form an unyielding body structure.

Growing feet prefer cotton, wool or mixture socks, but if you must buy stretch socks, then see to it that they don't need to 'stretch' much.

Feet need to be measured every month or so, but there are two rough and ready guides. Put the shoes on a hard floor surface, the heels touching a chalk line, and then draw a second line where the toe-caps come. Now ask their owner to stand with both heels on the heel line, and see where the toes come. There was a photograph showing a 13-year-old girl's big toes stretching over an inch beyond the toe-line – so no wonder her toes were drawn up in painfully deformed positions.

The other guide is to sprinkle talcum powder into each shoe, and shake them gently until the powder forms a film over the whole inner sole. Then very carefully insert the child's foot so that the powder is undisturbed until the foot is in place. Fasten it, and let the child walk about normally for a minute or two. Then remove the shoe equally carefully, and look inside. Usually the imprint of the toes can be seen at the end of the shoe. There should be $\frac{1}{2}$ inch of powdered area untouched, beyond the end of the toe marks ($\frac{3}{4}$ inch for us).

The specialist's last words were, 'I know how difficult it is, I'm a father myself, but parents should *insist* on proper footwear for the first eight years – and longer if they can.' As a fashion concession he saw no reason why heels should not be higher as children grew older (as long as the base was broad enough for support), but that they should always be long enough he was adamant.

The shop assistants I have spoken to all tell tales of children who have got their own way – parents have bought shoes which were the wrong length, width and design because their children made such a scene that they were unable to withstand the pressure in public. But, without exception, those same assistants said how much they admired the parents who had the courage to refuse to buy irresponsibly, however much noise and fuss the child created. Such parents, I was assured, maintained a quiet, unyielding front as they thank the assistant – and walk out holding a screaming, defiant child tightly by the hand (it never pays to give in to emotional blackmail).

Their observations are worth recording, because often it is fear of what assistants are thinking which is one of the reasons for parents capitulating.

PREPARING CHILDREN FOR REGULAR VISITS TO THE DENTIST

I recently heard a dentist tell of a 2-year-old with a mouth full of black decayed stumps where white milk teeth should have been, all because he was put to bed each night with a dummy dipped in blackcurrant syrup.

The best possible preparation for a visit to the dentist is to try to make sure that nothing needs to be done on arrival. But there is a happy medium between establishing good basic patterns of care, and becoming obsessive.

One mother said, 'I always scrape the jam out of her jam tarts, and if she goes out to tea I tell the mother that she is not allowed iced cakes or sweet biscuits. But lately she plays at nothing but "sweets". She takes her dolls shopping, buys them anything they want, encourages them to eat-up, and then smacks them quite viciously for being naughty. I'm beginning to wonder if I've gone too far.'

Yes! But fortunately nature came to the rescue by inspiring the sort of spontaneous play which helps resolve conflict, and restore a balance between inner and outer pressure. And the mother was sensitive enough to notice the danger signals, and allow the play to continue while she rethought.

Wise action begins with understanding the problem, and in the case of tooth decay the problem is plaque. This is a sticky, colourless, nearly transparent film which continuously forms on teeth. It is made up mostly of bacteria, along with saliva and food debris. When ordinary sugars come into contact with certain bacteria found in plaque they form acids. These acids begin the tooth decay process.

The best prevention against tooth decay is not to encourage an unnatural addiction to sugar, and to brush away the plaque after breakfast and at bedtime every day (the British

Dental Association accepts that fluoride toothpaste helps prevent decay). Children are natural mimics, so clean your teeth when you help them to clean theirs, and their identification with you will strengthen the habit.

By about 2½ years all twenty milk teeth are usually through, and this is the time to start regular visits to the dentist. Before that, children are welcomed as an audience while you go for a checkup. On these introductory visits it is best only to have an inspection, and perhaps a professional clean – and if you 'dread going to the dentist' keep it to yourself! Fear is catching.

Children need time to absorb new experiences, so don't ask anything of them on their first few visits, not even a ride in the chair. They just need to see you in a bewildering new setting, having a stranger doing things to your face and mouth, and to sense that you are all right and don't mind at all. Quite a tall order seen from their point of view.

When children are ready to accept a friendly overture from the dentist, then they can sit in the chair and look at the little tools of his trade. They may even be ready to let the dentist look in their mouths, but if not it can wait for another time. Confidence and trust grow slowly, and this is a relationship in which they are particularly necessary.

They must trust their parents, too, so beware of sweeping statements such as, 'If you clean your teeth you won't have to have fillings.' It may be true, but can't be guaranteed. If a filling is necessary be honest about that, too. The answer to 'Does it hurt?' is 'Yes, sometimes. But we all have to have it done, so we just have to be brave about it.'

FINDING THE COURAGE TO SEEK A SECOND MEDICAL OPINION

In Victorian times children were seen and not heard, and their parents – particularly their fathers – were presumed to be the unquestioned authority on their upbringing. Then came the swing of the pendulum and 'experts' were presumed to be the authority, with parents put in the position of children waiting to be told what to do. And now the next swing has arrived, with 'experts' telling parents that they are the experts on their own children.

This is all very well, but after years of having their confidence undermined it is very hard to know when to relinquish decision-making, and when to take it back again. And in no field is it more difficult than in health.

There must be few parents who haven't faced the dilemma of whether or not to seek medical advice. With parents' confidence being at an all-time low they are torn between the fear of not seeking help in time, and of being made to feel that they are 'fussy mothers or fathers'. In fact, very few doctors berate parents for leaving it too late, or condemn them as fussy, but that doesn't prevent parents *feeling* that they are being judged.

Doctors tell me that the opening gambit of most people (not just parents) is, 'I'm sorry to trouble you, but . . .'. The peace of mind that follows a visit is incalculable, and that together with a prescription is usually enough. But if it isn't, or if there appear to be side-effects, then do go back to report.

Sometimes, because doctors are human, and because some have greater experience and a closer affinity with, say, children or the elderly, you may occasionally have the gut feeling, 'He doesn't understand . . .', or 'She's not really listening to me . . .'. Or you may initially feel confident, but after carrying out the advice may suddenly say to yourself, 'This isn't working . . .'

I am a great believer in this sort of intuition, because I find from experience both for myself and others that more often than not it is to be trusted. At this point you stop handing over yourself, or your child, like a parcel, and start being responsible again; so go back to your doctor, offer your observations and feelings, and talk things over in the spirit of shared responsibility.

If you are still not happy, then think it over and either fix a deadline after which you will act, or go ahead and find the courage to go back and ask for a second opinon at a higher level.

Please understand that I am not inciting people to mistrust their doctors, or to be awkward, demanding or irresponsible. I am just saying that *sometimes* a parent really does 'know' more than a doctor can tell in the early stages. Sometimes parents only imagine that their child 'isn't quite right', but sometimes they are certain – and are eventually found to be correct. And the sooner hidden complications or handicaps of one kind or another are diagnosed, the more quickly the child can be helped.

Sometimes it is the treatment that parents query, for example prescribing drugs for infant sleeplessness over a period of time. Occasionally two or three good nights' sleep can break a habit, but if not then both the parents and child may need counselling and the kind of support that are outside the scope of some doctors to provide.

Just occasionally a particular doctor may say something like 'He'll have this all his life . . .', and any 'life' sentence needs to be seconded by a higher authority if parents are to believe, accept and learn to live with it – if only for their peace of mind. And sometimes such pronouncements prove to be wrong.

Sometimes constipation may need a prescribed laxative, sometimes advice on diet, but sometimes – if it is a prolonged history of holding-on to stools – it may be more appropriate to seek help from the Child Guidance Clinic than the doctor.

No one can be right all the time, but the final responsibility rests with parents. You are free to change your doctor, or to ask him to refer you to the paediatrician at the local hospital, or the Child Guidance Clinic. You can even write directly to the hospital or the clinic; they may respond by asking you to refer to them through your doctor, but at least you will then have their letter to take with you when you ask again.

Finding the moral courage to risk rebuff in the search for further help is part of parents' continued growth and development.

'DON'T TALK TO STRANGERS'

Not long ago I was taking part in a local radio phone-in programme dealing with the problem, 'How do you protect children from the danger of going with strangers without frightening them?' A local headteacher spoke of the excellent work done by the local police in schools, where they give talks and show films. He also went on to give an example of the wider co-operation between schools and the police.

Two 8-year-old boys were walking to school when a car drew up and a middle-aged man offered them a lift. They refused it firmly, and walked on briskly. The car followed, stopped again, and the offer was repeated. They had already worked out what they would do if this happened, and crossed the road to join a mother taking her younger children to school. As soon as they arrived they reported the incident to the headmaster, and gave him the colour and make of car together with its number. The police were informed and arrived at the school within minutes, getting from the boys an excellent description of the man. Within half an hour the car and owner were identified, and his address verified (he is now under surveillance).

The police then phoned all the local schools asking them to tell the children that a curb-crawler was in the district. The message was passed on calmly, and they were reminded not to go home alone (as routine now as the drill for crossing the road).

The discussion continued and various parents phoned in, and then a young man came on saying, 'Why are you afraid of frightening children? It was fear that kept me safe. We were shown a film at school where two kids were offered ice-creams, and got into the car, and then it went the wrong way and wouldn't stop. The last shot showed two gravestones with their names on in a churchyard. I was terrified, and suddenly knew what Mum and Dad had been on about. It wouldn't have been any good them just telling me – I wouldn't have taken enough notice. But the school alone wouldn't have been any good either, I should have thought, "Why didn't Mum and Dad tell me? Didn't they care enough about me?" It's got to be parents *and* school together.'

We agreed with him, and amended our thinking. Perhaps sometimes children do need to be frightened into safety, but by parents who are serious and calm, without clouding the issues by their own fears and emotions.

The rules the police themselves formulated for children, which are now issued nationwide by the Home Office, are these:

NEVER go away with a stranger. NEVER get into a stranger's car. NEVER accept sweets or money from a stranger. ALWAYS play with friends – never alone. ALWAYS be back home before dark. ALWAYS tell your mum or dad where you are going and when you will be back. If you are ever frightened, ask an adult lady for help – or go to a police officer.

Perhaps a final rule might be added:

IF you are lost, go into a shop to ask the way.

Bearing in mind the multiple hazards which threaten children's safety during at least their first six vulnerable years, we really do need to accompany them everywhere. Even taking and returning each other's children to play in homes just down the road. And long after that judgement is still needed about distance, route and reliability before we can decide when they still need us, or when their friends would be protection enough.

TEACHING ROAD SENSE

Road safety and road sense aren't quite the same thing. Road safety is our responsibility for children in the earliest years when we know they don't understand the danger. It means safety catches on gates, locks on doors and reins or holding hands out walking – and an extra burden of anxiety about stairs and lifts for those who live in high-rise flats.

But while we are being totally responsible for their safety children are already beginning to catch road sense as they absorb our attitudes towards roads and traffic.

Do we always go to the crossing, press the button, wait for the light, and then cross with deliberation? Or do we thrust the child in a flimsy buggy out between the parked cars far enough for us to have a quick look, before dashing over?

In fact, if you watch the faces of children who are poised in the road on the edge of fast-flowing traffic like this you are unlikely to see fear. They have such perfect trust in adults to keep them safe, and are so ignorant of danger, that they usually exhibit nothing but interest in the traffic rushing by, or else they are daydreaming quietly, lulled by the movement of their ride, and waiting for it to continue! But that is no excuse for us imprinting on their inward eye this dangerous method of crossing a road.

Once children are walking and talking the same considerations apply. On roads where there is no designated crossing do we say, 'Come on, quickly . . . over the road . . . hold my hand . . . hurry up', as we snatch, grab and stride off (causing little legs to run)? Or do we say, 'Now, slowly . . . let's just look first . . .'?

Children need to sense our caution constantly. As their understanding of words and experience grows we can invite their positive co-operation, 'I can see a car on my side, what can you see on yours?' They need to learn that 'traffic' is individual cars, bikes and lorries – each of which is dangerous in motion. Watch young school children crossing the road unaccompanied, and you will see some of them flicking their heads right-left-right as though they are performing some magic ritual which will then stop the traffic, render them invisible, or allow them to walk through it inscathed!

We must also be aware of the fact that children can't gauge speed; not only that, they have their own system of classification according to size. A big double-decker bus quite a long way away will be seen as a much greater danger than a sports car at the same distance.

Gradually we have to invite them to take over some of the responsibility, 'Now, you say when we can cross . . .', and either confirm their 'Now!' or say, 'I think we had better wait for the red car to go by, it's being driven very fast . . . there . . . it's gone!'

The hazard that remains is the fact that children's deep concentration focuses on one thing at a time. If the ball has rolled into the road, if a friend, a dog or an ice-cream van is spotted on the other side, then they fly straight as a crow to the object. They are not being naughty, careless or silly; it is simply a fact of life related to their stage of development and experience.

They don't really 'know' about road safety until they have a sudden fright – a horn blares, brakes are slammed on, tyres screech on the road, and suddenly the danger of roads becomes a reality. It is the moment every parent dreads. And it is why we have to go on holding ourselves responsible for our children's safety, and never assume they 'know' from telling and curb drill alone.

COPING WITH THE AFTER EFFECTS OF SHOCK

There are times in the lives of most children when they are exposed to shock. By this I mean that without warning something happens which is not only totally unexpected and frightening, but upsets the predictability of their secure world.

They may love and be confident with dogs, and although their parents hold their hand and say to the owner of a strange dog, 'Is he all right with children? May he be stroked?' the caution doesn't really register – until a dog snaps at them, or bites.

They love going past the Fire Station, and know (in theory) that engines and firemen are to put out fires, but fire holds no real peril – until the chip pan goes up in flames.

They are given kerb drill, know that traffic is dangerous, and are self-consciously virtuous about stopping at the kerb to look both ways, but they haven't a clue as to what being 'runover' is all about – until they dash after a ball, brakes squeal, horns blare, and they are rooted to the spot in terror (or worse).

They know that knives and glass are dangerous, and are more than familiar with our warning 'Be careful, you'll cut yourself', but the cutting of hair, nails and paper isn't anything to be bothered about, so they are only words – until they really cut themselves, and blood streams out to drop on the floor and stain their clothes bright red.

All these events can shock a child more than we realize, partly because of the suddenness, partly because of the consequence, partly because of the drama of the moment when something that they've 'been told' becomes reality, and partly because they also have to contend with our reaction. And just when they need us to be calm we are apt to shout or slap through a combination of fear and relief. But what happens next?

It is natural to be thoroughly frightened at the time and for a time afterwards, but then fear should give way to a healthy wariness rather than escalate to a state of heightened anxiety.

Once we have dealt with the emergency the natural impulse is to tell absolutely everyone about it, as a way of getting it out of our system and, sometimes, to convince ourselves that it wasn't our fault. This is helpful, as long as we are not so dramatic that we add to our child's fear and inhibit his own need to talk-it-out. But it helps both of us if we can manage to retell it, in his hearing, with our feelings well controlled, 'We've just had a nasty shock . . . (give the *facts* accurately and without blame) . . . we're both very shaken still, but Tom's all right . . . no, there was no damage . . . the driver was very frightened, too . . . In a way it's a good thing, it will make us very much more careful.'

We once came upon a road accident when our daughter was 5 years old. Ambulances and fire engines were on the scene, and the burned-out car had been towed into a field. She was happy with the reassurance that the occupants were safe, and that the ambulance had taken them to hospital just to make quite sure they were all right. But the burned-out car haunted her for weeks. She asked questions about fire every day, and couldn't go to bed unless we had let the fire die right down and put the fireguard in front of it. She wanted the ladder and the garden hose under her bedroom window, together with a bucket of water and a bucket of sand.

Everything she had been told about fires suddenly came together – the firemen's ladders and hoses, the fireguard indoors, the buckets of sand and water remembered from bonfire night. We complied with it all, and listened and reassured her as she stopped talking about the car and started to ask about almost everything else, 'And if we go in the train? And is it all right to go in the lift? Are we safe on the top floor?' Never have we been so familiar with, or grateful for, the fire regulations everywhere we went.

It took months for the nightly rituals to be relaxed, but eventually she talked and played her way through the experience, as children will if we allow them to keep the wound open (in their own time and way) until it heals from inside.

An understandable reaction is for parents not to talk about whatever-it-was, thinking 'It's best forgotten, and the sooner the better', but that isn't how children's minds work. They may not talk about it, especially if we create a conspiracy of silence, but that doesn't mean they have forgotten, only that instead of everything coming out it is being pushed down into their subconscious mind where it will remain as unfinished business, or come out later in disguised ways.

The greatest help we can give is firstly to talk about it to others in front of the children in a calm and reassuring way, and secondly for us to take our cue from them – if they want to talk we must listen, and reassure them calmly on all the points they raise. And if they want to 'play it out', to let them; even if the toy car is wrecked, it is a small price to pay for helping a child to work a fear out of his or her system.

Parents are comforting, but nature's inspired drive to play is usually the greatest therapy of all.

PART SIX

THE BEDROCK OF OUR LIVES, FAMILY AND FRIENDS

GRANDPARENTS

In the natural course of events grandparents and grand-children take to each other like ducks to water. For grand-parents there is the emotional blood-tie without ultimate responsibility – at the end of the day grandchildren can be handed back to their parents. For grandchildren there is the joy of doting grown-ups who are special to them, with time and patience to spare.

As their babies grow up, sometimes parents watch children and grandparents basking in each other's company with a pang of envy tinged with guilt as they think, 'I could be lovely and peaceful and patient like that, if I hadn't got this lot to do!'

It helps if grandparents can recall the times when they, too, were overtired, impatient, unfair and unwise. The clock can't be put back, but they can make up to their grandchildren for what their own children sometimes missed and this making-good is handed on from generation to generation.

Grandparents are noted for spoiling their grandchildren, but it isn't cuddles, stories, love and little treats that 'spoil' a child. What could be more natural than for absent grand-parents to enjoy keeping an eye open for things to take to the child who is so constantly in their thoughts? Scribbling pads, pocket toys, a fancy hairclip or cowboy hat, a book to share, an empty chocolate box filled with odds and ends, a home-made gingerbread man or a flowering busy-lizzie in a pot. Each visit builds up the child's expectations, and it is intelli-gence not greed that eventually prompts the opening ques-tion, 'Hello, what have you got for me?'

But how mortifying it is for parents!

It helps if just sometimes grandparents come empty-handed, and then the inevitable question can be met with, 'Nothing today, I've just brought me. What shall we do together?'

What does spoil a relationship, is for grandparents to undermine parents' authority. If parents say, 'No more, I think you've had enough,' then it is a recipe for discord if grandparents say, 'Oh, let him have another, he's only young once,' or, 'Here, love, have a bit of mine.'

Wise grandparents know both how to back-up parental authority, whilst retaining their own integrity in their own homes. One daughter-in-law said how grateful she was to her mother-in-law, explaining it like this: 'We have four under 7 and have to be strict if we are to cope. I was in a bit of a state with my first one, and too hard on her I think. She now bites her nails quite badly. Our rule is that everyone puts on their slippers before coming indoors. Gran's is that everyone wipes their feet on the mat, but needn't change shoes every time they dash in from the garden to show or ask her something. But she makes it right by explaining that as she only has Grandad to look after now she doesn't have to have as many rules as she did when her family was young. And also that their carpets are old and don't have to be taken such care of now. She manages to be *both* on the children's side, and ours, equally. So we all love and trust her.'

Grandparents have one very special claim to fame. However many times children are 'told', it takes a long time for it to sink in that their own parents were once small and had mothers and fathers of their own, and that these grandparents are the very ones they actually had. At this stage they lap up every anecdote that grandparents can remember, and stories of misdeeds are particularly appreciated.

Inevitably, after such a rewarding visit, children tend to be a bit difficult the next day – a little overtired and overexcited, but above all a bit flat. These are the natural reactions to anticipation, a peak of enjoyment, and a coming-down the other side; it hardly ever has anything to do with grandparents 'spoiling' the children.

Parents need approval, appreciation and support rather than advice – and there is no place at all for criticism. If the bond of love and trust is there they will feel free to talk things over if they want to before coming to their own decisions – if it isn't there, then such a relationship needs to be built up well before advice is even contemplated.

But as a *Woman's Realm* survey testified, there is an overwhelming vote of love confidence and gratitude flowing between the three generations in the vast majority of families.

MOVING HOUSE

The young and the old find it particularly difficult to move house because home is the one secure place within which,

and from which, everything else happens. Their most signifi-
cant memories are there, and at neither stage can they
imagine any future.

Younger parents are also likely to have some regrets about
moving, but by their example children can begin to learn that
'off with the old, on with the new' is no philosophy for living
either. Life should be an adventure, but with hope for the
future tempered by some regrets for the passing of the old
way of life.

If you are moving, talk to your children about your
impending move with the same loyalty; understanding, sadness and happiness that you would observe in talking about
the death of a friend, for that is what it may feel like to a
child.

When you start house hunting explain why this is necessary, not just once but whenever a natural opening presents
itself. Always allow sympathetic listening time to children's
questions and objections, and answer them honestly; there is
no guarantee that they will 'soon make new friends' or 'love
their new school'.

Take the children with you when viewing if possible. We
were amazed at our children's quick feeling for whether a
house was 'nice' or 'nasty'. Their reaction had little to do with
the furnishings, decorations or owners for many were empty.
They just seemed able to sense the atmosphere of a home. I
think we shouldn't discount the existence of deep instincts
underlying our rational judgements, especially in children
whose 'knowing' is sometimes clearer and more accurate
than our own.

If you need to park the children with friends or relatives
on the day of the move be sure that they have had several
days in which to pack, unpack and repack their personal
possessions in a large carton placed in their bedroom.
As they work at the task they will also be playing with the
idea of a new bedroom. And when they finally arrive at the
new house be sure that the unopened carton is waiting
for them so that they can work at settling themselves into
their new room as they worked themselves out of their old
one.

Your new house won't feel like home unless you have all
arranged and rearranged your possessions until they feel
right.

MAKING FRIENDS

Imagine that you are the child of giant parents: if you are 5ft. 5in. then your parents and their friends would be about 10ft. 10in. or more. You would, of course, be used to it, but wouldn't you greet someone of your own size with relief and enthusiasm?

This affinity of size is one of the bonds between children, but another is the ease with which they can communicate with each other, often without any words at all. Colour, class and language are no barrier when children play together. I have watched them in a country where the language is foreign, and have envied them their unselfconscious enjoyment in each other's company.

Their first playmates are usually the children of our own friends or neighbours, but these are not of their own choosing and the word 'friend' is not always appropriate, especially by my dictionary definition which says: 'One . . . joined to another in intimacy and mutual benevolence'.

The ability to make friends in later life is based on children's early experience of relationships in general, and perhaps even more on our attitude to their friendships. Our fears and prejudices can do more harm than the good we are trying to promote.

Welcome any child who plays with yours to their mutual satisfaction. Let them sort out their own squabbles with as little interference as possible, and come to an agreement with the other parents that you will be free to restore children to their owners (without recriminations on either side) on those inevitable days when it just doesn't work.

Remember, too, the attraction of opposites. The child from a gentle home often revels in a rough-and-ready environment, and vice versa. The child who feels the need to be aggressive at home may be an angel in somebody else's house or garden. The quiet child may shout in noisy company, and the noisy ones may enjoy unaccustomed peace and quiet. But the child who is bullied by older brothers and sisters may bully smaller children unless the adult on hand says at the first sign of it, 'It's all right, you don't have to fight here. Nobody's going to hurt you.'

Every friendship offers its own learning, and has its own natural duration. Our part in this is to make everyone welcome in our homes while the relationship grows through its own ups and downs, and to help children to accept the parting if it comes.

SOME OF TEENAGERS' OBJECTIONS TO PARENTS

I have only recently become aware that some of my readers are teenagers, so I wrote to a 14-year-old friend of mine who lives on Merseyside to ask if there was anything she and her friends would like me to write about on their behalf.

Back came a letter taking me straight back to adolescence, so accurately had she pinpointed the irritations and embarrassments.

I am sure Garnet speaks for many, and I hope you will respect her point of view as much as I do – and learn from her.

Garnet and her friends are sick and tired of the parental record that goes on churning out 'Who are you with, where are you going, what time will you be back, have you got your coat . . .' It was the last one that rang such a bell for me. When our son was 21 he was going off to a rather grand dinner-dance, the sort where a dinner jacket was worn in those days, and he blew in to say good-bye.

We were sitting by the fire, and I looked at him with enormous pride and satisfaction – but while my eyes were registering him as a young man, my mouth opened to say all the usual things I always said automatically whenever either of the 'children' went out. Before the words came he caught my eye, and with the friendliest grin said, 'It's all right. I've got my doorkey, and my clean hankie, and my dry nappy.'

Far from being hurt or angry I found it just right, and in the laughter there was learning – I *was* boring, it *was* time I asked myself why I did it, it *was* time I stopped making these mechanical responses.

Which of us hasn't said 'Good-bye. Have a nice time. Mind how you go/watch the roads/drive carefully'? It is self-defeating if it has become a ritual, because the irritation it sets up can bring about the very carelessness we are trying to avoid. So why do we do it? I suspect as a kind of safeguard for ourselves – if there was an accident our anguish wouldn't be compounded by guilt, we would be able to say, 'the last thing I said was . . .', and everyone would reassure us, 'Don't blame yourself. It wasn't your fault.' But we really mustn't clutter children up with our seemingly endless guilt complexes. There is a self-indulgence in this that needs to be curbed if we are not to bore and irritate our young into acquiring cloth ears in self-defence. As another teenager said, 'I like it when Mum and Dad show they care about me, but not when the things they say are just habit.'

And what about, 'Have you got your gym shoes . . . swimming things . . . homework . . . dinner money'? Playing at 'mothers' can become a way of life that doesn't help our children to grow up, though it may give us the emotional satisfaction of feeling needed. If children forget to take something to school, then they will miss a swim, or get into trouble, or go without dinner – and they'll gradually learn to remember. But learning will be easier if we say at teatime, 'Bad luck. You must be starving, we'll eat early' rather than 'Well, it's your own fault. I've told you enough times. I can't think of everything.' We don't really mean to say these things, they just slip out through habit – which sets up the ritual response. And before we know where we are the real learning through experience is lost in a barrage of pointless exchanges.

If we can cut down the number of stock replies we pour out at regular intervals, then it is (marginally) easier for Garnet and her friends to accept the questions that *have* to be asked – for the very simple reason that it is just possible the answer may be vital in an emergency.

The resented questions are usually Where are you going? Who will you be with? What time will you be back? Young people feel they are not being trusted. Actually, parents are much more likely to trust their children, but doubt the responsibility of others, or the pressures exerted by the group, or to fear an accident or frightening experience.

It is unreasonable to expect children of any age to know what it feels like to be a parent – even we didn't know until the baby was born – so a certain amount of resentment is something parents have to put up with. But basic rules for safety are something teenagers have to put up with.

All parents dread the idea of 'something happening' to their children, but these fears must be kept in proportion – they are going to make errors of judgement in all sorts of ways. There is no way of growing up except through their own experiences.

We just have to trust them – *and update our rules from time to time*, as their growing responsibility earns them greater principles.

BE WARY OF TOO MANY CLAIMS ON A CHILD'S TIME

Some time ago I met a happy, busy mother who, when asked how everybody was, said 'Fine, but Bill and I are worn out running our family taxi service!'

They had three children of 4, 6 and 9. The 4-year-old went to playgroup five mornings a week, to a different playgroup on two afternoons, had dancing lessons another afternoon, and regularly spent Saturday mornings with a friend.

The 6-year-old had spelling and reading homework every evening, plus piano, recorder, dancing and riding lessons out of school hours, and piano and recorder practice had to be done every morning before breakfast.

The 9-year-old was supposed to have half an hour's homework every evening (but it always took longer), piano and violin lessons, with practice each morning (he played the violin upstairs while his sister played the piano, then they exchanged places for her recorder and his piano), cubs, football on Saturdays and orienteering with his father on Sundays – after the whole family had gone swimming.

I was torn between admiration for their efforts to open up the world to their children beyond the television screen, and concern for the children caught up in an endless whirl of activity from dawn to dusk every day.

None of us can make judgements. I didn't know the family well enough to know whether they lived in a fifth-floor flat in a tower block, or in a family house with a large garden in a friendly neighbourhood, or in rural isolation. Neither did I know whether all the family shared their mother's vitality and usually inexhaustible energy. But I did wonder whether, if they stopped to think about it, everybody was happy with life as it was, or whether some of them were doing at least some of all those things because they thought they ought to, or to please someone else, or because they didn't realize there was any alternative.

I thought of another family I knew. The husband and wife were both doctors practising in a new town, but they decided this was no life for any of them because they had neither time nor energy to enjoy themselves or each other. So they moved to an isolated house on a Welsh hillside a few miles from a small country town, where the father joined a local practice. The two older children went to the village school, and the 3-year-old was at home with her mother. Both parents felt concerned about the isolation of their youngest, and settled her into the once-weekly playgroup to make friends.

Soon both mother and child felt part of the community, and the mother arranged for Kathy to be taken to play with a friend, or to have a friend home, on all the non-playgroup days. Often the children would stay with each other for the whole day, and sometimes another child would join them. As the mother was still trying to decorate, alter curtains and generally settle into their new home, the car-ferrying and entertaining became somewhat of a burden, but both parents felt it was the right thing to do. Until one day, when Kathy was getting into the car, she said, 'Do I *have* to go and play? Couldn't I just stay at home?' She could, and did.

Her mother said, 'I had been so busy feeling guilty, and doing what I felt was our duty, that I simply hadn't thought to ask Kathy what she wanted.' But Kathy knew exactly, she wanted to potter about by herself, doing what she wanted to do, in her own time and way. And so she did, with her playgroup morning and only occasional visits. She was one of those lovely self-contained children for whom the day is never long enough, happy to be with others sometimes, but just as happy to be alone because her inner resources were such that she never felt lonely.

The happy medium between under- and over-stimulation is hard to find. But once a child feels pressured, childhood is at risk – and nothing compensates for the loss of childhood.

PARENTS' FEAR OF 'UNSUITABLE' FRIENDS

One of the perpetual fears of parents is that their children will choose a group or gang of friends who might lead them astray. Most parents would be deeply distressed and ashamed if any child of theirs was involved when a gang of Hell's Angels decided to pick a fight with an opposing group; or was one of a gang of football hooligans who rampaged through streets inflicting damage on persons and property. Parents may also be anxious if their child sports weird hairstyles, wondering where it may lead; and others are upset if their child belongs to the 'gang' which monopolizes the climbing frame at the playgroup.

The dictionary definition of 'gang' is: 'a company of work-men, or of slaves or prisoners; band of persons acting or going about together, esp. for criminal purposes *or one dis-approved of by speaker*' (the italics are mine).

Somewhere between the criminal and our own prejudices we have to draw the line between what is permissible and what isn't.

Most gangs are just friendly groups of children who have the common bond of being in the same class, or street, or church, or youth club. They share common interests, and get on together better than with others in the same area.

But my heart goes out to the mother in a very tough area who said, 'Once our playgroup children go to school we know that by 7 – or even 6 – they'll belong to the gang and will start law-breaking. Well, you have a choice. Either your child joins the gang, or is bullied by the gang. Given that choice, you would rather your child wasn't bullied.' Many of you will belong to gangs, or 'bands of persons going about together'. Some of you will be Weight Watchers, or members of a fan club, or Bingo players, or on the Housewives

Register. And what's so wrong about that? You value your homes, and love your families, but sometimes you need to get away from the constraints they put upon you, and just be yourself.

So it is with children at each stage. They love you (never doubt that), and know from a very early age what you approve and disapprove of, but they too need to escape the constraints of 'family' sometimes and to feel carefree. They also enjoy the difference in other personalities and family patterns, so that they can begin to find their own individuality and preferences.

If home is over-quiet and calm, they want muddle and noise and action; if home is over-controlling, they want to break out a bit; if home is chaotic or aggressive, they want peace and quiet; if home is conformist, they want to look and sound outrageous; if home is indifferent, then there's real trouble, because instead of testing and finding the balance between opposites there is no 'home' but the gang.

It is pointless to tell parents not to worry, but if your child is one of a small gang – around six to eight – and you approve of most of them, then you have little cause for real concern. If all the home backgrounds were exactly the same there would be no testing, only reinforcement, of parental values.

It's true they will egg each other on a bit, and may do and say and wear things you won't approve of, for this is an essential stage of growing up. But in a small group, with one or two special friends for support, it is unlikely that the pressure of the others will lead children further than they want and need to go.

If any of you reading this are teenagers, may I offer an observation? On looking back I seem to have spent so many years being the sort of person I thought other people thought I ought to be, and now I wish I had had the courage to find myself sooner. I was afraid of losing the good opinion of others, and this kept me a goodie-goodie for too long. On the other hand I have worked with 16–18-year-olds long enough to see that exactly the same can happen in reverse – people can conform to the gang for too long, because they are afraid of losing the good opinion of their friends.

Somewhere inside, there is a part of you that is *you*. Listen to it, and don't do anything that strikes a warning note at this

deep intuitive level – however much courage it takes to say
No.

DEATH IN THE FAMILY

Even when children have been brought up in a family where
death is accepted as part of living, and where it has been
spoken about in an ordinary, as opposed to a 'special', voice,
it is still a shock when it happens to a pet guinea pig or
hamster. How much more shocking it is, then, when a loved
grandparent dies. How can we help? What do we say?

Try to put yourself in their shoes. They are almost always
aware when something serious is happening. Probably there
have been phone calls, in tones more anxious and loving than
chatty; conversations between husband and wife expressing
both their concern and caring; frequent visits to homes or
hospitals, with carefully thought-out little gifts. If so, then
there has been a period of preparation, but it is still a solemn
moment when death is announced in a family.

Do tell the children at once, even though you are crying. It
is right that deep emotions should be shown and shared, and
much less frightening than to have you shut yourself away in
silence or with still-audible sobs. Remember that for children
the emphasis is always on what is visible rather than invisible, so their immediate focus will be on you. And you will be
their pattern in this as in everything else. So let them know
that you grieve when you lose someone dear to you, and let
them see that tears are nature's way of helping us to cope
with the emotional overload, and let them kiss and cuddle
you better (which is the spontaneous way of comforting
someone that you have already taught them). And then be
brave – but not too brave – hugging them back, blowing
your nose, and sharing a pot of tea and some sweet biscuits.

Having shared the 'down' bit, then try to help all of you to
take an up-turn. This doesn't mean being artificially bright
and chatty, but just trying to restore everyone's sense of
balance a bit in order to face the days ahead.

Try to see what has happened through a child's eyes. If we
say, 'She just went peacefully to sleep and didn't wake up

any more,' then children may be frightened to go to sleep in case they don't wake up; they may even wake you up in the night to be sure that you haven't left them in this mysterious manner. If we say, 'He has gone to live with God,' then we face 'Where does God live?' and with all the astronauts now buzzing about in space this is very difficult to explain to the satisfaction of their very literal minds. Or they may say, 'But I don't want him to go and live with God, I want him to come and see me,' and I think we should accept their sense of anger (which is very common) at being left – it is such a compliment to the one they loved. The anger will burn out in its own time, especially if we say, 'Neither did I, and I shall miss him too.' If we say, 'The hospital couldn't make her better,' then a visit to Casualty or the Maternity Wing may hold real dread. It helps to keep things in perspective for them if we say, 'Almost always the doctors and nurses can make people better. But just sometimes they can't, especially if they are very old.'

Or, if the death was of a young person, 'Just sometimes when people are born they aren't quite as strong as us and they die more easily.' It is best not to say more than children are ready to take in, just answer their questions as they arise, not only honestly, but in such a way that their own fears are quietened.

One of the first questions may be 'Will I die?' or 'Will you die?' and the only honest answer is 'Yes, one day – everybody is born and everybody dies.' If the next question is 'When?' it is helpful to explain that small pets live for about two years, and cats and dogs for about fifteen years, and people for about seventy years. Facts help to reduce fears. If a specific condition has been mentioned, such as cancer, then explain that doctors are making new discoveries all the time. Truth, hope and reassurance need to go hand in hand.

Another natural question is, 'If you died what would happen to me?' And you can explain the domestic set-up which would be probable. Some of you might want to add that you would always be with them even if they couldn't see you, but since the thought of invisible people watching them wherever they go, and whatever they do, can be upsetting, do explain that it is your love, not 'you' which would be with them, even as the legacy of love their grandparent had for you all will stay as part of the family.

SOME OF THE REASONS FOR SCHOOLGIRL PREGNANCIES

Every stage in our lives has its origins in the stage that preceded it, right back to childhood. We don't ask to be born, we don't choose our parents, and some people have more difficulties to overcome than others. But we need to understand how some of the problems can affect teenagers if fewer babies are to be brought into the world without two parents and a home (of some sort) to welcome and sustain them.

Girls become pregnant for all sorts of reasons, some conscious, others subconscious. But there are certain patterns which recur, and if we understand some of the underlying reasons better, then the parents of today's babies might be able to prevent at least some future unhappiness.

It is fashionable at the moment to say that no girl need become pregnant if she says No, or if she takes contraceptive precautions – which is a bit like saying that no one need lose their temper if they count up to ten. Our emotional lives are more complicated than that, and if I change their names I can use real girls to illustrate some of the complexities of schoolgirl motherhood.

There was Alison, the adored only child of older parents. They were firm over good manners and homework, but otherwise asked nothing from her. She grew up to be a beautiful sunny child, loved by everybody, and loving towards everybody – she just accepted that people enjoyed doing things for her (which they did), and never knew it was possible to reverse the situation. Until she discovered she could make a particular man happy by giving herself to him in a way which was new to her – but because it made her happy, too, she just assumed it was right. Even the baby felt right, as did her mother's taking-over the baby after birth.

This is dangerous innocence, and it is deeper than lack of sexual knowledge: there is a time and a place for 'doing what comes naturally' – but not if it means that no thought has been given to the consequences, and no responsibility is accepted for the outcome.

There was 14-year-old Janet, who bitterly resented her mother because she felt she had never been loved or cared for. Her mother went out to work (which was accepted as necessary), but when she came home she still never found time for Janet. So she found herself a boy friend, became pregnant, and arrived at the Child Guidance Clinic because her mother 'couldn't get through to her'. But Janet had it all worked out in her own mind, and one day explained it with devastating simplicity, 'Mum never did a thing for me. Well, now she'll have to – because I'm not going to do anything. And if the baby dies it will be her fault, and then perhaps she'll be sorry.'

Linda also had an unloving mother, but she found a different solution. She knew how babies were made, and set about getting one for herself, 'Because now I shan't be lonely any more. I'll have someone of my own to love, and who'll love me.'

Peggy felt that what she was doing was wrong, and didn't really want to do it – but she was afraid of losing her boy. So she did nothing, except allow herself to be pulled to pieces with fear, guilt and anxiety, until her periods suddenly stopped. And by then the decision had been made for her – she was going to have a baby, and the entire course of her life had been changed for ever.

Libby had never been any good at school, but it did wonders for her confidence to discover that she was good at something, and her ability to attract boys saved her from feeling a failure in life. She loved being one of the crowd, and they told her nothing would happen if she did it standing up, or went to the loo straight afterwards. But they were wrong.

Janice certainly didn't mean to go too far, and was confident that neither she nor Colin would even do such a thing – but they had reckoned without the tidal wave of sexual and emotional response which swept away their resolve one evening, leaving them both frightened, guilty and remorseful. And Janice pregnant. Other Janices and Colins have their resistance lowered through alcohol, and then say, as one did when asked if she had had sex education at school, 'Oh yeah, but you don't think about that when you're doing it, do you?'

And now some young unemployed girls feel that they might as well have a baby – it's better than hanging about doing nothing.

It isn't enough to approve, or disapprove, of girls who risk handicapping their children's future and their own by bringing them into the world for any of these reasons. We have to accept our share of the responsibility – the quality of love, and quantity and quality of time, we give our babies, toddlers and growing children has a direct effect on their attitude to love, sex and their own babies.

TEENAGERS' REACTIONS TO PARENTAL CRITICISM OF THEIR FRIENDS

My 14-year-old friend, Garnet, from Merseyside, asks me to explain how she and her friends feel when parents criticize their friends. On their behalf she writes, 'They don't even know them, and yet they make judgements. They always like the ones we don't, like the goodie-goodies, who we find a bore, and anybody a bit way out or trendy they suspect of being up to no good.'

Most parents would accept the honesty of this, but justify it on the grounds that the possibility of children being tempted into premature sex or pill-popping (either for kicks or contraception) now exists as a genuine threat. They know how 'right' either can seem if the case is put persuasively enough by someone a little older who is loved or envied for their confidence. And how much worse it can seem to be thought a goodie-goodie than to give in, or accept a dare 'just once'.

It isn't surprising that parents want to protect their children's childhood, and steer them clear of those who look as though they could lead them astray. And most of us can remember occasions in our youth when we were secretly glad that our parents put their collective feet down hard on some friendship or escapade that secretly scared us.

But before we pat ourselves on the back, or our children on the head with exasperating condescension, we had better listen to the next bit of the letter. It goes on, 'They criticize your friends – "not good enough, common, poor homes, funny mother/father/cat/dog/football team – look at their front garden, speaks volumes, doesn't it?" Seriously, when our friends are criticized we go all hot under the collar.' And we really can't wriggle out of this one. As John Cleese said on a recent television programme about jealousy and anger, 'If these feelings don't come out honestly at the time they get bottled up, and come out later in sneaky ways.' Like our petty criticisms which hide our bottled-up fear of sex or drugs? It is very understandable, but I think we should look at it from another angle.

I was talking with a group of mothers, asking if any of them could recall anything their parents said which still has a direct bearing on their lives, even though it was illogical. And one said, 'Yes. When I was about 6 I was walking along the road with Mother when she said, "You can tell what sort of woman lives *there* by the milk bottles on her step – she's a slut!" I looked at the bottles, and saw they hadn't been rinsed clean, and that word "slut", said in that tone of voice, has stayed with me ever since. I'm neurotic about milk bottles. I've even started out somewhere, and have had to go back just to check them. And it's silly, because if they are immaculate I can go off quite happily, even though the beds are unmade and the washing-up isn't done.'

If we are too rigid in our standards we inhibit our own growth as much as our children's. If we are too trendy we may offer no real anchorage, and instead of bobbing about and flowing safely for a while with each successive tide, they just may become part of the flotsam or jetsam of damaged lives.

I remember taking a succession of best friends home, from earliest childhood onwards, only to see some of them with new eyes when our parents received them so warmly. Many of them they genuinely liked, and those who didn't fit in anywhere with anything Mother made allowances for, and explained how this or that might have come about.

I can still hear Father saying, 'You shouldn't talk about people', and Mother saying, 'But if I don't explain how shall they understand?' I have always been grateful for those wise and loving insights.

But I also admire the parents who made their daughter's latest boyfriend welcome, tried to like and understand him, made allowances for his home, upbringing and divorce, but still couldn't trust him. One day they sat their daughter down and said, 'Now, love, listen . . .', and told her all their observations and misgivings. Then they said, 'Now, you know how we feel, and why. But it's your life. We won't refer to this again, but whatever you decide, if you need us we're here.'

TWO LEVELS OF FRIENDSHIP

The other day a friend complained to me that her 18-year-old daughter had slammed the front door on her boyfriend, and announced to her mother that she 'wasn't going to be spoken to like that'. The result was that he had called to apologise the next night and had taken her out to a very expensive restaurant.

I said, 'How splendid!' and meant it, remembering myself throughout the years, endlessly enduring silently or pretending to enjoy myself because I had been brought up not to hurt anyone's feeling: frozen feet at football matches, when the game bored me to tears; hearty tramps of fifteen miles, when five was much more my mark; Bernard Shaw's plays at the stage when I loved musicals, and later, musicals when I was hooked on Shaw.

I thought of all the hurtful comments, the accusations, the broken dates, the boy who took me to a dance and didn't dance with me once, and heard myself saying endlessly, 'It's all right, it doesn't matter – honestly!'

It couldn't have been more dishonest. Or more damaging. The strain of bottling up our feelings, of endlessly denying our own inner needs, of constantly holding ourselves responsible for everyone else's happiness, is physically, mentally, emotionally and spiritually exhausting. It is also damaging to those whose feelings we imagine we are saving. How can people grow up to be thoughtful and caring if no one ever lets them know when they have overstepped the permitted limit?

Although I agree with the mother that her daughter had been rude, it also looked as though a 'rude awakening' was what the young man needed at the time. And he had the grace to apologise, and make amends. So far so good. The relationship is now on an even keel for a while, but the testing time isn't over, especially for the girl. Door slamming paid off handsomely the first time, and it may be tempting to try it again. But next time the boy may feel he wasn't in the wrong, and stay at home waiting for *her* to apologise and make amends.

She may have what it takes to cool off, even to know in her heart that she had gambled on the same tactics being success- ful a second time, and go round to say she is sorry. On the other hand she may not be willing to admit, even to herself, that this second time she was behaving like a prima donna rather than acting instinctively as she did the first time.

She may even justify herself along the lines of, 'Well, I can't help it. That's the way I am. That's me.' Which is nonsense from adults as well as adolescents. It may be the way we are at the time and we can't help many of the circumstances that led up to it. But it isn't the full and final version of 'me' speaking, and since we have a good measure of free will we have to decide whether we are going to stay as we are, or accept the pain of continuing to grow and develop as long as we live.

From the toddler stage onwards we need two concurrent levels of friendship. We all need personal friends of our own choosing. Some will be so similar that they reinforce us; others so different that they stimulate us, and bring to the surface new aspects of ourselves; some may be from a different background, teaching us to value people for what they are even if their homes and lifestyles are different; and some will be going through the same experiences, reaffirming that we are not alone or 'different'.

At another level we need people in our lives we can trust, respect and look up to, though we couldn't call them friends in a familiar sense. They are the ones who stand by, without judgement, lectures or taking sides. Who will listen and understand, and share thoughts and insights when asked to do so, but will stop short of offering 'advice'. A creative relationship helps people to work out their own solutions, and to learn from experience.

PREPARING TO ANSWER PROFOUND QUESTIONS ABOUT DEATH

One afternoon as I was setting the tea table our 8-year-old son said, 'What does being dead mean?' It was one of those profound questions that children ask when they *really* want to know the answer. And there can be no fudging about the reply, it has to be given in the same spirit of honesty as that in which the question was asked.

I knew he wasn't asking about physical death, he was already fully acquainted with dead flowers, dead flies on the windowsill, dead birds and mice in the garden, a dead cat and two of her kittens. So he was asking what happened to the life that once animated what has died.

The immediate answer could only be, 'I don't know. Nobody knows, though different religions have their own beliefs.' And then, in one of those flashes that sometimes come out of the blue, I suddenly knew what I believed.

The day before I had taken both children to London. At one point we found ourselves outside the BBC, looking up at all the windows and wondering which belonged to which programme. We chose one for 'Listen With Mother', one for the News, and one for every other programme we could think of (we didn't confuse the issue between radio and television). Remembering the man who had so recently installed our first television, twiddling knobs to find stations and adjust the focus, volume and brightness, it was suddenly both easy and truthful to say I thought it might be rather like the television programmes. We knew where they came from, and we knew that if our set was all right we could see them. We also knew that if something was wrong with the set we might not be able to see them clearly or even at all, so then we had to send for someone to put it right. But there might come a time when the set was beyond repair, and not even the most skilled attention would produce even a flicker of life out of it. At that point it could be buried in the nearest rubbish skip, or burned, or disposed of in any other way since it was of no further use.

But the fact that our particular set was dead wouldn't alter the fact that the programme was still very much alive, still being beamed-out in invisible waves through the air just as it was before – only now we couldn't see it.

I don't know whether I was right or wrong, but it seemed enough to take him over the deadness of dead, and left all the options open.

I also know that the concept is still valid for me, and I am content not to know more than I can sense as yet.

If you have a religious belief, whatever that religion may be, then you will want to pass it on to your children as it came to you.

For others, it is less easy. But we must never rob anyone, let alone children, of the confidence to *live*, through fear of death (whether it is from illness, old age or the bomb), for that is a waste of the life that we have.

Not all parents believe in God, but sensing their children's vulnerability they may at least be able to say of death that they 'don't know, but feel sure it will be all right'. Since nature has ordered the seasons, and all that goes on in them, so predictably and miraculously, why shouldn't there be more to life than we know about yet?

If children find their own explanations then that is best of all for they will be literally made to measure, from the child's own experience and imagination. A 4-year-old found just such an explanation for the death of a dearly loved and very old friend, 'She was just used up, wasn't she?'

Whatever we say at the time when these profound questions hit us, we should go on thinking long afterwards. At every stage our children challenge us at the deepest level of

our thoughts and beliefs, and in trying to meet their needs
they offer us unlimited opportunities to grow up ourselves.

OPTING OUT OF RESPONSIBILITY

I was shopping in Sainsbury's recently when a family caught
my attention. There was a baby in a buggy, a child of about 3,
a large comfortable dad pushing the buggy, and mum with
the wire basket. They were all standing by the shelves of
tinned meats, and I heard mum say, 'Which one shall we
have? Her husband said good-naturedly, 'Which ever one
you like,' to which she replied, 'Well, there's that corned beef
at 72p, this one at 85p, and that other one at 83p. Which do
you think?' to which he responded with mild exasperation,
'How should I know? Any one.'

Nothing is ever as simple or obvious as it may seem, and
I fell to wondering about this exchange. Increasingly I see
couples shopping together, not just young families but old
age pensioners, and youngsters possibly sharing a flat
together. Some couples pick up various joints to discuss and
examine them for weight, price, quality and fat distribution;
some compare the prices only; some buy a week's supply,
balancing the budget between an expensive joint and cheaper
cuts. But all these couples take a lively interest in what they
are doing.

The older couples tend to have a different pattern, the
husbands patiently pushing the trolley while the wives plan
for the cheap and tasty meals that our mothers cooked for
us – neck rings of mutton casseroled with vegetables, belly of
pork with apples and onions, stuffed breasts of mutton, liver
with bacon pieces.

But the family buying corned beef didn't come into any of
these categories. The woman seemed to want to hand over
all responsibility to the man – the question, 'Which one?'

wasn't a lively enquiry, it was flat and somehow indicated that she didn't mind which he chose, as long as he did the choosing. Various explanations came to mind; she could have dreaded making any decision if she had the sort of husband who criticized everything she did – but that didn't seem likely. She could have been feeling so tired or ill that she had no mental energy available for even the simplest choice; she didn't look either, but if she was in the early months of pregnancy that could certainly have accounted for her lack of enthusiasm for shopping for anything, let alone corned beef. They could have been on such a tight budget that every penny counted, but she wasn't comparing weight with price – and in any case there are forms of protein that are better value for money than tinned meat. She could have been so unhappy or worried that she didn't care about anything. Or – and this is the thought that came to mind – she just could have been one of those people who never take responsibility for anything, if it can possibly be avoided.

This is one of the hazards of fathers choosing to become more involved with their families – the danger that they may find themselves being asked to shoulder (rather than share) yet more responsibility. Right down to deciding which brand of corned beef.

There is a lot of talk these days about the importance of giving children choices and responsibility for making decisions. But this can be taken to excess just as easily as it can be denied.

No one, whatever their age, wants to be responsible for every choice and decision throughout every day – and anyway it isn't practical. And no one should want to avoid all responsibility.

Some mothers who choose to stay at home with their young children (usually because they want to be the ones who help their children to acquire these and other skills for living) may find that their decision-making in the home becomes too strong and over-confident – and then fathers wanting to take an interest can be put-down so many times that *they* eventually opt out. This is the reverse of the couple in Sainsbury's, but it is just as much a hazard.

Bearing all these pitfalls in mind we need to recognise that there are times when every member of a family should be able to feel it is safe to be dependent sometimes, and equally safe to be independent too – then, between these extremes, everyone can also learn the art of inter-dependence.

THE INHIBITING FEAR OF WHAT OTHER PEOPLE MIGHT SAY

On looking back some of us may remember how as children we worried over just about everything: homework, getting on the wrong bus, being too late or too early, too fat or too thin, being left out of things or making mistakes and being found out. In short, a general state of anxiety in case we were 'wrong', if not a continuous sense of impending disaster.

Becoming parents ourselves may open a whole new chapter of worries about the baby, beginning with fear of suffocation, pneumonia, germs and accidents, and going on from there.

Most people find a better perspective with age, a few never quite shed the burden, and some of us can remember a specific moment when we let go. For me it came on a small stony beach in France many years ago.

A truly enormous woman shed her cotton dress to reveal a bikini, and precariously lowered herself down on to a very small beach chair to sunbathe. My upbringing indicated that if you were that size not only did you not wear a bikini, you didn't even wear an upholstered one-piece bathing costume; you just hid in tentlike dresses, and pretended you didn't want to swim or sunbathe, in case you offended anyone. But on this lovely family beach no one even noticed, they were all so happily and naturally enjoying themselves.

The smallest children pottered barefoot over the stones without a toy between them. They filled yoghurt pots with stones, then tipped them out to fetch water, then dropped stones in, then filled empty shoes with stones, or sat in the water, or were just loved and talked to. No one shouted, no one smacked, no one cried.

Then a group of teenagers arrived to sunbathe and talk, to be joined at intervals by others. Everybody leaped up to greet each newcomer with the customary kiss on each cheek. How lovely! No one was made to feel plain or left out. Finally a one-legged man in bathing trunks swung into view on his crutches, and all my worries returned. Suppose his crutches slipped on the stones? How would he get into the water? How would he get out again? And how could he find the courage to do all this in public? He had no such worries. He reached the water's edge, threw his crutches up the beach, and hopped barefoot over the stones until he was deep enough to flop in. He swam for ages, then paddled into the shallows on his arms, hopped out and swung off to lunch.

It was a revelation. A whole beachful of people quietly living their own lives as they wanted to live them – while I was striving to live mine according to everyone else's expectations of me.

We are all influenced by our upbringing, but at some point we have to accept responsibility for our own lives, and try to live in accordance with our own truths and values. Then things begin to fall into place.

We still worry sometimes, but only over genuine problems, and as a dog worries a bone. We chew it over, then leave it alone, then return to it with new insights, and give it another chew. Eventually the problem resolves itself and we know what we are going to do.

Those who find it difficult to stop worrying may have been brought up to be overobedient and self-sacrificing. But it is a denial of the self that is uniquely ours if we constantly deny it expression. Children need us to be ouselves in order that they may become more fully themselves.

Children need us to build up their self-esteem so that they feel adequate rather than inadequate, in control of events as often as possible instead of at their mercy, and lovable rather than unacceptable. They also need our help in learning how to go about problem solving.

But remember that the worries children have are huge at the time, so listen carefully until you have really understood what their problem is before helping them to resolve it to their satisfaction.

Then they won't have to use valuable energy in wasteful worrying.

INTRODUCING YOUNG PEOPLE TO CHILDREN

Many schools are now running courses to help teenagers to get to know and understand children. The idea gained ground as the divorce rate shot up; so many young parents felt that they had married too soon, had children too soon, and didn't know what they had let themselves in for until it was too late. Even if the ideal of 'every baby a wanted baby' came to pass it still won't help much if, once the baby arrives, the full-time care proves to be an endless uphill obstacle race.

So, the thinking went, if boys and girls could be taught something about child development, and work and play alongside children in playgroups, nurseries and mother and toddler clubs, then at least they would know a little about children. And if they did they wouldn't feel like the desperate teenage mother who battered her baby, and then broke down sobbing, 'I loved him so, only he didn't love me. He used to wait until I sat down for a minute, or fell asleep, and then cry deliberately to make me get up again.' She truly thought a newborn baby was capable of this kind of deliberate plotting.

Other parents accept that babies can't help crying, yet at the toddler stage they are hurt and upset by what they see as deliberate testing 'just to be difficult'. If they understood a little about the way children grow and develop they would know that the 'terrible twos' is a stage when children try to find out where the limits are set, and that they haven't yet learned to control their emotions. Toddlers want things NOW, and they hate, fear and love with total intensity at the time of arousal. This is not because they are wanting to test and punish their parents, but because they are trying to 'find out', and their parents are their sounding board and their yardstick.

These school classes come under various names such as child development, home and community or family studies. They used to be offered only to girls, but now boys take them too with great success, particularly when it comes to being with the children. Boys often seem better able to relate to children as people, rather than as live dolls to be cuddled and mothered, and their own delight in brick-building and model-making reduces the children to awed spectators, and then encourages them to enthusiastic DIY efforts.

A bachelor in his late twenties recently spent three days with a film crew in a playgroup. He couldn't get over it, he kept saying, 'All these little people, busily getting on with their own little lives!' He had had no experience of children before, 'Except that I saw them at bus stops and around in general, just sort of being a bit of a nuisance – but there they were, all those little *people* . . .'

At first these 'preparation for parenthood' classes were confined to the less able children, while the more academic classes got on with their studies, a situation which makes no sense at all. *Everybody* needs to understand children, whether or not they choose to marry and have some of their own, because to learn about the growth and development of children is to learn about ourselves.

The enthusiastic teachers of these classes all say that the discussions are as invaluable to them (personally) as they are to the boys and girls. The young have wonderfully lively minds when they are interested, and they connect all that they hear with their own childhood, and their own parents. Memories of childhood joys, sorrows, angers and fears come thick and fast, and then when they have been with the underfives they come together again with growing insight to talk about what they have seen.

Inevitably they discuss their own parents – with touching loyalty, but nevertheless with a real need to compare notes. They discover that a great many parents are over-controlling or over-protective, but they also learn that those children whose parents have switched-off and leave them to their own devices are to be pitied, not envied. They can understand and put up with quite a lot of overprotection and control, but still wish their parents would sit down and discuss some of their rules and update them from time to time. But what they dislike above all else is constant, habitual, automatic, boring, pointless nagging. And being shouted at.

What emerges more clearly than anything else is that children who are loved, made to feel secure, responsible and valued, and grow up with the idea that mistakes are not to be feared but to be learned from, are the truly privileged members of our society.

WHOSE CHILD ARE YOU?

Whose child are you? You may well be great-grandparents in your seventies, with a parent – or even both parents – in their nineties. If so, you will probably be in no doubt that they still regard you as their child! My mother died last year, in her ninety-second year, but her greetings to me on my weekly visit rarely altered; if she was feeling down she would say, 'My darling child . . . how glad I am to see you', and if she was feeling fine she would say, 'Darling, how tired you look, come and sit down'. And on those days I was in no doubt that I was indeed still her child, because no matter how bright and lively I had felt on arrival, this maternal solicitude was the beginning of the draining away of my energy – until in the end I did indeed feel like a tired child, while she drew strength from looking after me.

But there were many other days when we talked and laughed together, and recharged each other's batteries, just as people – not mother and daughter at all – and with no allowance made, or needed, for age. On those days neither of us felt the need to 'look after' the other, the maternal role was shelved for both of us. And the freedom was delightful.

I suspect this is the way it is for many of you. Just as it is also the pattern for others to be aware that in their parents' presence they always feel a child again, and the struggle remains to go on trying to find the courage to be true to themselves – even if it brings the inevitable reprisals, and the consequent feeling of guilt.

There will also be those of you who feel the full maternal (or paternal) responsibility for parents who are frail or incapacitated in some way – and others who are put in this position not by love but by manipulation. Yet others may find themselves in this position through being too dominant, having worn down the resistance of parents who couldn't hold out against them, even though they didn't want to lose their independence. And some of you have painful memories of parents who were either missing from your lives, or who let you down. The greatest let-down of all is to feel that you weren't loved – and yet there have been letters from such 'children' telling me how they have come to understand that it was genuine love, not lack of it, which prompted their parents to resort to adoption, or made it impossible for them to show the love they felt.

The overall message is that there is no such thing as the perfect parent, but that the parents each child has are the ones they want most. They don't ask us to be perfect parents, they just ask us to be *their* parents, the ones who love them whatever they do, or can't do.

Also, that marvellous people have emerged from the most unlikely homes, and that some haven't been able to take advantage of loving and stable homes. Parents are not responsible for everything!

We can only be the parents that our own parents, our temperament and genetic inheritance, and our life's experience, have made it possible for us to be. We all have to start from where we are on the day our children are born. There can be no oughts, or musts, or shoulds – we just have to do our best each day, learning from experience, comparing notes with other parents, and picking up tips and insights wherever we can. And this is how the *Woman's Realm* column 'Your Child and You' came to be conceived. We saw it originally as something quite practical and down to earth, with a weekly topic centred on the under-fives (with the occasional one relating to the fives to tens). We didn't want to offer 'advice' because that would be impertinent; we also knew that neither I nor anyone else could be right for everyone, and that even those who found it helpful certainly wouldn't agree with everything. All of which felt right, because no one must take away parents' responsibility for doing their own thinking, and making their own decisions for their own children.

But nothing in life stays still. Between my growing understanding of my own relationship with my mother and father, and all that you have told me about yourselves and your own parents (letters from men and women, from the ages of 14 to 74) and your children, we now know that the phrase 'your child and you' has constant echoes and repercussions from the cradle to the grave.

No one is an 'expert' in this field – people have been trying to work out how lives, societies and civilizations should live since the beginning of recorded history.

But we can at least go on trying to help each other.

PART SEVEN

SOURCES OF SUPPORT AVAILABLE TO PARENTS AND CHILDREN, LEADING TO SCHOOL ENTRY

THE NATIONAL CHILDBIRTH TRUST

The birth of a baby is the simultaneous birth of the parents. No matter how carefully they have been prepared for the event, there is no way that they can anticipate how they will *feel* when it happens. There may be an instantaneous rush of love and protectiveness that is overwhelming in its intensity; there may be an inexplicable feeling of nothingness, as though all the emotional switches had been turned off; there may be a sudden wave of sadness behind the joy, a feeling that nothing will ever be the same again (it won't), and that the 'self' is cut short before its time (it isn't).

One of the first pioneers to regard birth as an event of equal physical and emotional importance to both mother and child was Dr Grantly Dick-Read. Early in the 1950s one of the mothers most grateful for his help and guidance through the pregnancy and birth of her second child was Prunella Briance. Wanting to make his skills of relaxation, deep breathing and support during labour more widely known to women – and eventually more widely practised by doctors and midwives – she put an advertisement in *The Times* saying that he would speak at Caxton Hall on a certain day. Over a hundred people turned up to hear him speak, and out of that audience about a dozen joined Prunella and decided to form what is now the National Childbirth Trust.

It is only natural that any enthusiastic gathering of 'amateurs' should arouse concern in relevant professional bodies, especially when the focus of attention is mothers and their unborn babies. But parents had so much to offer each other that there could be no going back on the inspired idea of bringing together on neutral ground all the professions concerned with birth, together with parents and prospective parents.

There are now 300 branches throughout the country, with an evergrowing number of parents able to support each other in different ways.

Antenatal classes help parents to look forward to their baby's birth with confidence and understanding. A fee is charged for the course, which includes preparation for breastfeeding, discussion of common procedures during labour and birth, information on which drugs may be offered, and advice on caring for a new baby. Classes are kept small to encourage discussion, and fathers are invited to at least one, if not all, of the sessions.

After the birth, through the local branch network, new mothers are put in touch with members who have children of their own, and who are willing to help as much, or as little, as is needed. Whatever the problem – difficulty in breastfeeding, depression, loss of confidence, lack of sleep, the shock of a handicapped child, having to cope alone without a partner – there is almost bound to be someone available who has been through it all before. And who knows that to listen with understanding is the first stage of help needed.

Even if all goes well and there are no problems NCT is still an invaluable way to meet people with similar interests, and the groups organize outings, speakers, get-togethers for parents and children, babysitting services, social events, workshops and conferences.

At national, regional and local level the shared experience and learning builds up between general practitioners and midwives, paediatricians and obstetricians, physiotherapists and psychologists, statisticians and sociologists, biologists and teachers, together with the 'lay' people, each with an equal say on the subject of preparation for both birth procedures and postnatal support.

Increasingly NCT members go into schools, sometimes to bath, change and feed their babies as well as to talk about being a parent. One of the most hopeful aspects of this natural approach to parenthood has been the attitude of reverential wonder with which the teenagers (boys as well as girls) have shyly drawn near to the quiet corner where the baby is being bathed and fed. There is something about a baby that inspires hope for us all.

MOTHER AND TODDLER CLUBS

'Well, we shan't see *you* for a while!' the group said as a heavily pregnant mother strapped her toddler into the pushchair at the end of a Mother and Toddler Club session. But they did. Two weeks later she was back, having pushed her toddler and the new baby nearly two miles from her home. The mothers were concerned (and had a whip round later to send the little family home by taxi), but understood exactly when she said, 'I had to come. I live for Tuesdays. I'd never get through without you all.'

The explosion of these groups over the country testifies to the need parents have to come together with other parents and children. Often they are far away from their own parents, and are lonely. They need to share their problems and day-to-day difficulties, and to discover that they are not alone. They need somewhere to go where their children are welcomed and provided for by people who understand what toddlers need.

Some have lost their confidence after weeks or months in isolation, especially if they knew nothing about children before having their own. Others are happy and confident but long for a social occasion to look forward to once a week, 'Something to dress up for' as one put it, and 'Somewhere to speak at your own speed, and have a laugh' another said.

For many it is a relief to see their child with other children, and to discover that they come in all shapes, sizes and temperaments, with widely differing abilities at different ages and stages – and the same goes for parents! They and their children can then settle down to accept and enjoy each other.

Part of this enjoyment is seeing the children play and watching their reactions to all the toys and activities. Ideas are taken home that make the next week easier and happier.

These groups may be sponsored by the social services, a local church, a voluntary body, an individual, or a group of local parents. But the recent rapid expansion has been pioneered by individuals or groups associated with the Pre-school Playgroups Association, whose network of support reaches most parts of the country.

Each group is different, and if there are several in your area it is best to visit them all before choosing one. They vary in size, and noise, and the degree of organization. Some have visiting speakers, some run things 'for' mothers, others wouldn't exist at all unless everyone who could lent a hand, thereby becoming involved and starting a new stage in their own lives.

With encouragement the feeling of involvement which

comes to mean so much grows naturally and easily for, unlike a crèche, each child has to be accompanied by a parent or regular parent substitute (granny, nanny, childminder) who is responsible for him or her at all times. The friendships formed are often lasting, and the parents' presence gives the children confidence to play first alone, then alongside others, and to accept other adults.

The charges are usually modest, often just enough to cover the cost of refreshments, though some include a contribution to the rent of the hall or room, and expendables such as paint, paper and dough.

Many Mother and Toddler groups have a flourishing social life, with excursions, discoes, barbecues or family outings. Others run discussion groups for parents who want to learn more about children and being a parent. Joining one can benefit the whole family.

THE PRE-SCHOOL PLAYGROUPS ASSOCIATION

The Pre-school Playgroups Association (PPA) 'exists to help parents to understand and provide for the needs of their own children'. Its purpose isn't just to encourage playgroups where children can meet each other for friendship and satisfying play – important though that is. It certainly isn't to 'get them on' in any formal way, for that robs them of their childhood and defeats its own ends. It exists to help parents to become involved with each other, as they work and learn together to provide for their children's play and other needs.

Although this is the aim, it isn't the rule. No two playgroups are alike, not all of them involve parents, and if they do it may be formally or informally. With any luck you may have a choice, so do visit them all before you decide which one is right for your child *and you*.

Children's basic play needs don't vary. They need a warm relaxed atmosphere, neither imposed silence nor an exhausting noise level, in which they feel safe and happy. They need sand, water, dough, clay, paint, dressing-up clothes, a home corner, floor and table toys, books, climbing apparatus, and music-making in one form or another. Everything should be clean and in immaculate order, with the children taking their share of responsibility for this. They need plenty of adults who have time to sit down both to talk and listen to them, to tell or read them stories and to be available to help if they are needed.

But parents also have needs. Many welcome an opportunity to see how other people cope with squabbles, shyness, aggression and all the other difficulties of learning to dare and share. Others need play ideas that don't cost a fortune, or the confidence to tell stories, or to sing with their children (who won't mind a bit if it is out of tune). Many have skills to share, some rusting through lack of use, others as yet undiscovered.

Where better to learn and pass on all these things than in a playgroup, where the feeling of being accepted, liked and needed does such wonders for morale?

It takes courage to become involved, but there are very few who regret taking the plunge. For most it marks a new beginning in their own lives, and the one comment I hear more than any other is, 'If anyone had told me this time last year that this is what I would be doing now, I'd never have believed them!'

NATIONAL CHILDMINDING ASSOCIATION

Every day of the week 100,000 children are looked after by 50,000 registered childminders, and you may be contemplating adding to that number if – for one of many reasons – you really do have to find a daily home and mother substitute for your child. If so, how do you go about it?

Before doing anything, try to put yourself in your child's place by recalling your own early childhood feelings about your parents. I hear the same wide-ranging memories again and again, 'She was warm and safe and you could always go to her with everything'; 'She was a cold sort of person, but

Dad was quite different'; 'I think she loved us – I'm sure she did – but I never really felt loved'; 'Mum and Dad were so wrapped up in each other they never had much time for us'; 'I don't think either of them liked children much, they just wanted to get on with their own lives, so it was always Gran I turned to'; 'Mum was a great nagger and moaner, but she had to bring us up on her own so I suppose it wasn't surprising'; 'It was my dad I loved'; 'Mum had to go out to work, so we just accepted it – but on looking back I feel I missed out a bit'; 'Mum always worked, but we knew she loved us.'

You can probably identify with one of these comments, and know people who fit into the other categories – and if you do, you will know that a child's emotional well-being depends upon feeling loved, valued and secure. So your child's emotional welfare should be your first concern.

Some children need a lot of cuddles and demonstrative affection, and they will be happiest with a loving cuddly childminder who will supply that particular need in your absence. Other children are independent and so busy that they haven't got time for cuddles, so find someone who has the temperament to enjoy these sturdy individualists. Some children are rip-roaring monsters, and they need someone who can recognize the need to set limits with loving firmness without looking upon the behaviour as 'naughty'. ALL children need love, fun, fairness and security – and plenty to do. Not only toys, sand, painting, dressing-up and stories, but shopping, cooking, washing-up, mud pies, gardening, and all the activities of home-making that lay up a hidden store of memories on which they will draw when they become parents themselves. Incidentally, I see this as the greatest strength of childminders: no institutional care, however good, can give children these early patterns and impressions of home-making and mothering on which our lives are based.

Bearing all this in mind try to find a home that is similar to your own, for then your child won't be pulled between two widely contrasting patterns. If you live in small warm comfortableness, then your child may feel lost in a large bare house with three or four children: if you are meticulously tidy, then your child may come to love the freedom of a different home, and find the weekends restricting.

Parents should no more dream of finding somewhere just to 'put' their child while they go to work, than they would buy the first pair of shoes they saw without trying them on for comfort and style, comparing them with others, considering the matter carefully and finally asking the price.

You are making two decisions which will affect your child's life – the first, to work (about which there may be little or no choice); the second, to find a substitute mother and home of such worth that your child will still be able to look back on a happy childhood.

Because you love your child you will find both the time and the courage to visit all the registered childminders who have vacancies in your area (the social services will give you their names and addresses). And when you are invited in you will be brave enough to ask questions about what the children do all day, what they play with and where, what they have to eat and drink, what happens if they misbehave, what happens if there is an accident or they are taken ill. Only when you feel satisfied that this is the right home for your child has the time come to ask about cost and other practicalities, but at that point do listen carefully to what is said.

In 1977 the National Childminding Association was formed, and there are now 10,000 members dedicated to improving their services to children and parents. From my knowledge of them since its inception I can say with certainty that far from thinking your questions cheeky, they will heave a sigh of relief and say 'Thank goodness for a parent who *cares*'.

CRÈCHES

If you wanted an hour and a half to do a quick and efficient shop-up, unencumbered by a baby in a pram and a toddler, would you leave them in a dark and dirty hall, with a splintery floor, dirty toilets, few toys, thirty or more children, and in the sole charge of someone who had a record of child abuse? Of course you wouldn't – knowingly. But it could happen, if you thought the word 'crèche' meant something official signifying quality. And if you took the smiling welcome at the outer door at face value when you paid your money at 10.30am and were told, 'Don't worry about them, they'll be fine once you've gone. It's best to say good-bye here, it upsets them less that way. Go and enjoy your shopping. They'll be ready for you at 12.15 – don't be late!'

Most parents would ask to see the room first, but some wouldn't. Not because they don't care, but because they either have blind faith in 'experts', or because they quail when confronted by an authoritative figure and don't quite like to ask to see inside.

Anybody can set up a crèche, without restrictions or safe-guards, as long as it operates for *less than two hours* – and 1 hour 59 minutes is far too long for any child to be left without physical and emotional protection.

If a crèche operates for *more than two hours* at a stretch, then it must be registered by the social services. This means that the premises will have been inspected for safety, light, warmth, space, toilet and cloakroom facilities, and suitability of equipment and toys. There will also be a responsible adult for every 20 children, and at *least* two adults at all times. Registered crèches are often permanent, running daily, or two or three times a week for working parents, or shoppers.

Other crèches operate for one day a week, often in conjunc-tion with Further Education classes. If the course lasts all day, then the crèche must be registered. But if it is for a single class running less than two hours, it may not be registered, and needs to be looked at much more critically. For example, the children may be in the care of a single adult, even in another building to the one where the parents are having their class. If so, then there is no means of contacting the parents of those children who may have an accident, be taken ill, or become upset at the separation.

Crèches are also set up as a one-off effort for a day event, such as a conference or study day. Since some of you may well become involved in one of these it is worth considering the planning in some detail. Check the room for obvious dangers, electric sockets and flexes, unguarded heaters, french windows with ordinary glass, sharp corners at face level, dangerous substances in accessible cupboards, doors with low handles through which children could escape. Check fire precautions, and make sure that there is a first aid box. Know where the crèche is in relation to the parents.

One adult to six children isn't too many. Some of these can be boys and girls from the local school, or students, but a nucleus of parents is advisable. Parents should be prepared to go to their child immediately if they are wanted, not only in their own and their child's interest, but to prevent the upset escalating to the others.

Make sure that there is adequate insurance for the day, for both children and the premises. Work out the costs carefully to cover the premises, helpers, food (if appropriate) and expendables (paint, paper, dough, tissues). And do make sure that there is enough to keep the children happily occupied.

Ask each parent to bring a list, headed with the child's name, and giving information such as likes/dislikes, dos/don'ts, any family word for wanting to pass water or have a bowel movement, and sleep times (best adhered to if possible). Be sure that arrangements for lunch are clear and let it be known that 'special' things (including blanket pieces, and potty if necessary) are welcome but *must be labelled*.

Arrange for the helpers to be there 20 minutes early at least, so that there is time for introductions and settling-in.

After attendance at a crèche don't be surprised if your child is clinging for the next day, or even two.

THE TOY LIBRARIES ASSOCIATION

The mother of two handicapped children found toy buying particularly expensive and frustrating. Her boys would ignore some toys completely, or be bored by them very quickly, or become frustrated because they were too complicated, fiddly or fragile. Or they would become so deeply attached to one that it was subjected to constant use, often very rough, which led to great distress when it broke under the strain.

One day she was discussing this with a friend in a similar situation, and said, 'Why don't we try swopping one or two things?' The first swop was a small tough trampoline for a sturdy doll's pram. And bliss reigned in both homes for hours.

The circle of bringers and borrowers grew, and Jill stored the growing collection of toys in a large cupboard under her stairs. On a given day each week the house was full of parents and children trying things out, chatting and making friends, and finally deciding which toy to take home.

The collection outgrew the cupboard, and the space under their bed. Eventually premises were found to set up a permanent base where people could come to browse and try out a selection of strong, carefully chosen toys, register, then borrow one or two for a fixed period which could be renewed if desired.

The idea caught on, and because the principle on which they work is the same as a public library they became known as Toy Libraries. They vary, but generally charge a nominal fee for membership, with a modest 5p to 10p for the loan of each toy.

Although the first libraries were primarily for the physically and mentally handicapped, including adults, many are now open to anyone, from toddlers to senior citizens, including childminders, playgroups and one-parent families. There are over 1500 toy libraries throughout the country with more opening all the time.

Some are organized by voluntary groups in a wide variety of buildings; some are mobile; others are in community centres, special hospitals, schools and clinics.

The Toy Libraries Association doesn't run these libraries, but they maintain up-to-date records of all toy libraries that are in contact with them. A phone call or s.a.e. will give you the details of those in your area.

At first parents were so afraid the toys might be damaged that, having borrowed them, they tended to keep them safe on a top shelf! But slowly they have come to trust the librarians who assure them that toys are to be played with and enjoyed, and that inevitably there will be loss and breakage from time to time. The borrowing charge goes towards repair and replacements, and parents are encouraged to return broken toys, or bits of toys that turn up weeks later in forgotten pockets, under the bed or out in the garden.

In fact damage is very little for everything is subjected to rigorous testing by children themselves, for durability and play value, before being put in the library. Toy designers and manufacturers have co-operated to invent, improve and strengthen toys and equipment in the light of this practical experience. And based on this lively and informal research the TLA now produce an excellent *Good Toy Guide*, updated each year, which recommends over 700 toys chosen from the thousands examined by the TLA's Advisory Panel of experts and approved for their play value, with durability, design and safety taken into account. But above all each has been play-tested for three months by children themselves, monitored by a member of the Panel which has been testing toys for ten years.

NATIONAL ASSOCIATION FOR THE WELFARE OF CHILDREN IN HOSPITAL

Every year 800,000 children in this country have to go into hospital; one of them just could be yours. So do think about it before it happens, because you may need time to consider your reactions, and to prepare yourself.

For example, what would you do if you found you were 'expected' to go in with your child, and stay; or if the attitude was that you were 'expected' to observe restricted hours, or at least not be 'allowed' on the day of the operation?

The Government recommendations have been clear since the 1959 Platt Report on the Welfare of Children in Hospital, which indicated how important parents are to children while they are patients. Hospitals are 'expected' to have unrestricted visiting, and to encourage parents to stay with their children for as long, or as often, as they can.

It helps to know this and if your particular hospital doesn't encourage it, then you can ask to be admitted to another hospital (if there is one). If there is no alternative hospital then the backing of the Government recommendations, and the support of the National Association for the Welfare of Children in Hospital (NAWCH), may give you the courage to say quietly but firmly, 'My child needs me. I am a calming, not a disruptive, influence. If you have no space I will sit on a chair by the bed, though a mattress on the floor would be very welcome. But I am not abandoning my child to this frighteningly unfamiliar experience without the comfort of my presence.'

Some hospitals forbid visiting on the day of an operation, but sometimes parents have proved to be the most calming influence of all during the stages of preparation and the journey to the theatre. After the operation Government policy is that parents may be present when their child wakes after any kind of operation and for as long as he or she is conscious.

It is hard to insist, but if you feel strongly that you need to be there when your child regains consciousness you have the backing of the law. A High Court judge found that children in hospital should remain 'under their parents' care and power of control'.

Sometimes parents say they can't be with their child, but if the importance of their presence is explained they are often able to reorganize their lives in such a way that at least a daily visit is possible. If not, then someone loved and familiar may be able to be a substitute.

Sometimes nurses advise against frequent visits because 'They upset the children so', but this is to misunderstand the nature of the 'upset' and also of 'being fine'. A child may burst into tears of relief when a parent appears, and tears of distress at parting, but at least this indicates that the child is aware of the other world of home, and wants to go back there. It is distressing but healthy. Whereas sometimes 'being fine' means that there are no tears or any outward sign of distress because the child has withdrawn into himself in silent mourning. If this stage goes on for too long the next stage may be a blotting-out of home and parents, and an apparent adjustment to hospital life – he seems perfectly happy and makes friends with everyone. But then the transfer home can be distressing, for he may hold-back from letting himself go again with the old familiar trust and love, and family relationships may be difficult to re-establish.

It really does pay, especially for the underfives, to stay in or to visit every day, and to endure the distress with a firm, 'I'm going now, but I'll be back tomorrow.' But you must keep your word. If you can't be back until Wednesday, say so, and tell the ward sister so that the question, 'When is Mummy (or Daddy) coming?' can be met with a confident, 'On Wednesday when you have had one more sleep and one more breakfast.' It helps if you can leave your handbag behind, removing only your keys and money.

Tell your child honestly what is going to happen in general terms before he goes in. And then prepare him simply and honestly for the other stages just before they happen (the idea of an injection doesn't need to be dwelt upon for too long). Be honest about pain or discomfort, but explain that everything that happens is part of getting better.

There are some helpful books and leaflets available, including some in Urdu, Bengali, Punjabi, Hindi and Gujarati, which can be obtained from NAWCH. (See *Useful Addresses*.)

SCHOOL AT 4 OR 5? THINK ABOUT IT CAREFULLY

Children's age of entry into school varies quite widely across the country. The law states that all children shall be in full-time education when they are 5, and this is sometimes interpreted as being the term before their fifth birthday, and sometimes as the term after. But the law is quite clear, no child *has* to go to school until they are 5 – and not even then if the parents can prove to the authority's satisfaction that home education is being undertaken regularly and adequately.

This needs to be said loud and clear, because some parents are allowing themselves to be pressured into sending their children earlier against their better judgement. Where does the pressure come from? It is difficult to say, but some springs from an understandable belief (not always justified) that an extra year will put the children well ahead. An old countryman I knew used to say, 'If you 'urry 'em forrard, you'll backen 'em.' This can be as true of children as of plants.

Entry into an 'ordinary' admission class isn't to be confused with entry into a nursery class, nursery unit or nursery school, which may be a special addition to the local school. This nursery education will be supervised (ideally) by a specially trained nursery school teacher, with nursery nurses as assistants, so that there is one adult to every 13 children, unlike an ordinary staff ratio of may be one teacher to 30 children. Do ask if you are not sure what your local school offers.

It bears repeating, no one *has* to send their child to any kind of school before they are 5. If parents are enjoying their company, and they have plenty of friends of their own age, and plenty to do both indoors and out, then it is a pity to hurry them into regular attendance anywhere for five days a week before they are 5.

If, on the other hand, parents feel that their child would enjoy playing with other children for two or three hours once or twice a week or even more often after a while, then part-time attendance at a playgroup, or in flexible state nursery provision, may be a happy and valuable experience from about 3 onwards (especially if parents are involved with their children).

But it is *optional*. It is also unlikely to benefit children unless it is suitable to their individual age and stage.

All this was brought to my attention recently because in several areas now parents and teachers are coming together to consider the all important transfer from home to school.

As always, happy and confident parents follow their instincts rather than allow themselves to be pressured. Many enjoy being involved with their children in playgroups, but don't want school before 5.

Others are less confident and are full of doubts and fears. If they don't accept a proffered place at 4, or $4\frac{1}{2}$, will they be acting against their child's best interests? Some of the children are happy in playgroups, but will the teachers take it out on them if the offer of a school place is turned down? (No, many teachers understand this fear and go out of their way to reassure parents.) Would it be best to have one term in playgroups to get them used to a group, and then transfer them? (Two transitions, and two groups of children and adults to come to know, are just too much for some children. Their confidence is undermined just when it needs to be boosted.)

But it is the third group who give the greatest cause for concern. In almost all areas there are parents who are desperate – they wanted children, but the reality of living with them night and day is just more than they can cope with. They may have had too many children too quickly; they may know nothing about children and be unable to keep them happy and amused; they may be unable to manage money, and know little or nothing about nutrition and cooking. The result is that their nervous systems are frayed, and tears and temper alternate with an unpredictability which adds still further to the insecurity of their children. In areas like this parents may jump at the chance of getting their children into school as soon as possible after their fourth birthday.

It is to the credit of such parents that many of them would be hesitant about putting their children into day care (unless they were working), for it smacks of being 'a bad parent': but they would gladly hustle them into 'school' and 'education' because that smacks of being 'a good parent'.

It is understandable that some local education authorities should try to make provision in schools for these children, 'in response to parents' request', but it is doubtful if 'ordinary' school will help in the long run. These are the children of exhausted parents who are likely to have missed out on being played with and sung to, who haven't had a chance to explore, touch, smell, look, construct or play creatively, because the opportunity wasn't there; either because of their physical environments or because of innocent ignorance as to what children need.

These are the parents and children who need to make good all the missed stages in play and sympathetic relationships, and there is no way they are going to be ready to learn new skills (especially as complicated as reading, writing and numbers) until all the missed stages have been made good. And this means drawing the parents together as well as their children, so that with the pressure taken off they can learn to enjoy each other and meet each other's needs.

Even when children are ready for school there are still some teachers who expect too much of some children too soon. It is unreasonable to expect children to tackle this major transition in their lives, and to do homework in the first term, even if it only consists of 'looking at a book' taken home from school. School is school, and home is home, and few children can make a carry-over from one to the other in that first term. And they are so tired at the end of the day, and even more tired by Friday – most just want to go home and forget about school while they take up their old life again for relaxation.

Don't expect anything that first term beyond a happy settling-in, the making of friends, the making of a relationship with their teacher, and the confidence to go into school with courage and a feeling of importance and responsibility each morning. The rest will follow.

But if you live in an area where there is only one intake a year, and you are offered a choice of school at 4 years 1 day, or 5 years 1 day, do think very carefully – especially if there is a journey, and if entry into a large class isn't geared to the nursery school age and stage. Only you know your child, so visit the school, and then make up your own mind about what is right for *your* child under these circumstances.

APPENDIX 1

Useful Addresses

Action Against Allergy
43 The Downs
London SW20
Tel. 01 947 5082

Advisory Centre for Education
(ACE)
18 Victoria Park Square
London E2 0PB
Tel. 01 980 4596

Allergy Support Service
Chris Dowsell SRN
Little Porters
64a Marshalls Drive
St Albans, Herts
Tel. 0727 58705

Anything Left-handed
65 Beak Street
London W1R 3LF
Tel. 01 437 3910
(Catalogue, send 26p stamp.)

Association of Child
Psychotherapists
Burgh House
New End Square
London NW3
Tel. 01 794 8881

Association for All Speech Impaired
Children (AFASIC)
347 Central Markets
Smithfield
London EC1A 9NH
Tel. 01 236 3632

Association of Parents of Vaccine
Damaged Children
2 Church Street
Shipton-on-Stour
Warwickshire CU36 4AP
Tel. 0608 61595

Association for Spina Bifida &
Hydrocephalus
22 Upper Woburn Place
London WC1H 0EP
Tel. 01 388 1382

Association for Stammerers
86 Blackfriars Road
London SE1 8HA

Asthma Research Council
St Thomas's Hospital
Lambeth Palace Road
London SE1 7EH
Tel. 01 928 3099

British Association for Early
Childhood Education (BAECE)
Montgomery Hall
Oval
London SE11 5SW
Tel. 01 582 8744

British Institute for Brain Injured
Children
Knowle Hall
Knowle
Bridgewater
Somerset TA7 8PJ
Tel. 0278 684060

Your Child and You

British Migraine Association
178a High Street, Byfleet
Weybridge
Surrey KT14 7ED
Tel. 093 23 52468

Catholic Marriage Advisory Council
15 Lansdowne Road
London W11 3AJ
Tel. 01 727 0141

Child Growth Foundation
2 Mayfield Avenue
London W4 1PW
Tel. 01 995 0257

Child Guidance
(Local address available from telephone directory, or child's school.)

Children Need Fathers
18 Green Lane
Grendon, Atherstone
Warwickshire CV9 2PL
Tel. 08277 2427

Church of England Children's
    Society
Old Town Hall
Kennington Road
London SE11 4QD
Tel. 01 735 2443

Community Health Foundation
188 Old Street
London EC1V 9BP
Tel. 01 251 4076

Community Education
Open University
Walton Hall
Milton Keynes MK7 6AA
(Produce a series of parenting packs
including 'Childhood 5–10'
and 'Education Shop'. Write for free
catalogue.)

The Compassionate Friends
6 Denmark Street
Bristol BS1 5DQ
Tel. 0272 292778
(Mutual help for bereaved parents.)

Down's Children Association
3rd Floor, Horne's Premises
4 Oxford Street
London W1N 9SL
Tel. 01 580 0511

Dyslexia Institute
133 Gresham Road
Staines
Middlesex TW18 2AJ

Family Network
(National Children's Home phone-in
Service for families under stress.)
Tel. 01 226 2033

Food Watch
Butts Pond Industrial Estate
Sturminster Newton
Dorset DT10 1AZ
Tel. 0258 73356

Foundation for the Study of Infant
    Deaths
5th Floor, 4 Grosvenor Place
London SW1X 7HD
Tel. 01 636 7866
(Especially cot deaths; befriends
bereaved parents.)

Gingerbread (for one parent
    families)
35 Wellington Street
London WC2
Tel. 01 240 0953

Health Visitors Association
36 Eccleston Square
London SW1
Tel. 01 834 9523

Hyperactive Children's Support
  Group
59 Meadowside
Angmering
West Sussex BN16 4BW
(Please enclose a foolscap (9in x 4in)
stamped addressed envelope, other-
wise a reply cannot be sent back.)

National Association for Gifted
  Children
1 South Audley Street
London W1Y
Tel. 01 499 1188
(Voluntary counselling services for
parents.)

Invalid Children's Aid Association
  (ICAA)
126 Buckingham Palace Road
London SW1W 9SB
Tel. 01 730 9891

National Association for the Welfare
  of Children in Hospital (NAWCH)
7 Exton Street
London SE1
Tel. 01 261 1738

Left Handed by Post
Noddfa Lydart
Monmouth NP5 4RN
(Catalogue, send 26p stamp.)

National Autistic Society
276 Willesden Lane
London NW2 5RB
Tel. 01 451 3844

Mama (Meet a Mum Association)
Mary Whitlock
26A Cumnor Hill
Oxford OX2 9HA

National Childbirth Trust (NCT)
9 Queensborough Terrace
London W2
Tel. 01 229 9319

MENCAP
National Society for Mentally Handi-
capped Children and Adults
117–123 Golden Lane
London EC1Y 0RT
Tel. 01 253 9433

National Childminding Association
204/206 High Street
Bromley
Kent BR1 1PP
Tel. 01 464 6164

MIND
National Association for Mental
  Health
22 Harley Street
London W1N 2ED
Tel. 01 637 0741

National Council for the Divorced
  and Separated
13 High Street
Little Shelford
Cambridge CB2 3ES
Tel. 0923 22181

Mothers Apart from Their Children
  (MATCH)
c/o BM Problems
London WC1N 3XX
Tel. 01 892 9949

National Council for One Parent
  Families
255 Kentish Town Road
London NW5 2LX
Tel. 01 267 1361

Your Child and You

National Eczema Society
Tavistock House North
Tavistock Square
London WC1H 9SR
Tel. 01 388 4097

National Marriage Guidance Council
Herbert Grey College
Little Church Street
Rugby, Warwicks CV21 3AP
Tel. 0788 73241
(Leafets and books.)

National Society for the Prevention
    of Cruelty to Children (NSPCC)
67 Saffron Hill
London EC1
Tel. 01 242 1626
(If you know or suspect a child is
being ill-treated or neglected tell
your local NSPCC at once – to delay
could be fatal. The number is in your
local telephone directory.)

National Step-family Organization
Maris House
Maris Lane
Trumpington
Cambridge 0223 841 306

OPUS (Organization for Parents
    Under Stress)
26 Manor Drive
Pickering
Yorks
Tel. 0602 819423

Parents Anonymous
North Islington Welfare Centre
6–9 Manor Gardens
Holloway Road
London N7 6LA
Tel. 01 263 8918
(Listening and advice for desperate
parents.)

Patients' Association
Room 33
18 Charing Cross Road
London WC2
Tel. 01 240 0671

The Pre-school Playgroups
    Association
Alford House
Aveline Street
London SE11 5DH
Tel. 01 582 8871 or 582 8920
(Also for information about Mother
and Toddler Clubs)

Samaritans
(If you have a problem and need to
talk to somebody you will find the
number in your local telephone
directory.)

Stillbirth and Neonatal Death
    Society (SANDS)
Argyle House
29–31 Euston Road
London NW1 2SD
Tel. 01 833 2851

Stillbirth and Perinatal Death
    Association
15a Christchurch Hill
London NW3 1JY
Tel. 01 794 4601

Toy Libraries Association
Seabrooke House
Potters Bar, Herts
Tel. 0707 44571

The Twins Club Association
Mrs D. Hoseason
Pooh Corner, Steele Road
London W4
Tel. 01 994 1660
(For parents who have multiple
births.)

Women's Aid Federation
374 Gray's Inn Road
London WC1
Tel. 01 837 9316
(If you are a woman wanting to get
away from a violent relationship.)

APPENDIX 2

Booklist

1 Books for reference and dipping into from birth to late adolescence:
Jolly, Dr Hugh, *The Book of Child Care* (London: Allen & Unwin, 1985; pbk, 1986).
Leach, Penelope, *The Parents A to Z* (Harmondsworth: Penguin, 1983).

2 Family Relationships:
Cleese, John and Skynner, A. C. Robin, *Families and How to Survive Them* (London: Methuen, 1983).
Maddox, Brenda, *Step-Parenting: How to Live With Other People's Children* (London: Unwin Paperbacks, 1980).

3 Books on the emotional problems of growing up:
Crabtree, Tom, *The A to Z of Children's Emotional Problems* (London: Unwin Paperbacks, 1983).
Crabtree, Tom, *The Search for Love* (*Cosmopolitan* Magazine Books Offer; Venddek Mailing Ltd, 8 Holyrood Street, London SE1 2EL).
Lawton, Anthony, *Parents and Teenagers* (London: Unwin Paperbacks, 1985).

4 Books on play:
Crowe, Brenda, *Play Is a Feeling* (London: Unwin Paperbacks, 1984).
The Good Toy Guide, Toy Libraries Association (see *Useful Addresses*)
Jameson, Kenneth and Kidd, Pat, *Pre-School Play* (London: Unwin Paperbacks, 1986).
Marzollo, Jean, *Superkids: Creative Learning Activities for Children 5–15* (London: Unwin Paperbacks, 1984).
Marzollo, Jean, *Supertot: A Parent's Guide to Toddlers* (London: Unwin Paperbacks, 1984).
Marzollo, Jean and Lloyd, Janice, *Learning Through Play* (London: Unwin Paperbacks, 1984).
Matterson, Elizabeth, *Play With a Purpose for Under-sevens* (Harmondsworth: Penguin, 1970).
Playgroup Activities, Pre-school Playgroups Association (see *Useful Addresses*).
Williams, Sarah, *Round and Round the Garden: Illustrated Finger Games* (Oxford University Press, 1983).

5 Books with their own brand of insight:
Axline, Virginia, *Dibs: In Search of Self* (Harmondsworth: Penguin, 1971).
Lev, Mary and Dorling, Bronwen, *Rising Five* (Oxfordshire Education Department and Pre-school Playgroups Association). Obtainable from B. Dorling, 320 London Road, Oxford.
Lewis, Catherine (ed.) *Growing Up With Good Food* (London: Unwin Paperbacks, 1984).
Wakefield, Tom, *Some Mothers I Know: Living with Handicapped Children* (London: Routledge & Kegan Paul, 1978).